CBSE X 2020

10 SAMPLE PAPERS

Social Science

CBSE X 2020

10 SAMPLE PAPERS

Social Science

Includes
CBSE Solved Paper 2019

CL MEDIA (P) LTD.

Edition : 2020

© PUBLISHER

Administrative and Production Offices

Published by : CL Media (P) Ltd.

A-45, Mohan Cooperative Industrial Area,
Near Mohan Estate Metro Station,
New Delhi - 110044

Marketed by : G.K. Publications (P) Ltd.

A-45, Mohan Cooperative Industrial Area,
Near Mohan Estate Metro Station,
New Delhi - 110044

ISBN 978-93-89310-82-5

Typeset by : CL Media DTP Unit

For product information :

Visit :- **www.gkpublications.com**

or

Email :- **gkp@gkpublications.com**

CONTENTS

- 1 - 12 | Sample Question Paper 1
- 1 - 10 | Sample Question Paper 2
- 1 - 9 | Sample Question Paper 3
- 1 - 10 | Sample Question Paper 4
- 1 - 10 | Sample Question Paper 5
- 1 - 12 | Sample Question Paper 6
- 1 - 11 | Sample Question Paper 7
- 1 - 12 | Sample Question Paper 8
- 1 - 10 | Sample Question Paper 9
- 1 - 10 | Sample Question Paper 10
- 1 - 14 | **Solved Paper 2019**

PREFACE

2019 Board exams for Class X have ensured one thing - the paper pattern is going to be tricky at times but lengthy all the same! As we had predicted, the slight change in difficulty level of the questions asked was apparent, but numerous students mentioned that completing the paper in 3 hours was a challenging task.

The toppers, however, highly recommend practicing with Sample Papers so that students focus on answers and not get tired with writing. To ace the Social Science exam, it is crucial to get your basics right. This book has, therefore, been designed to help you maximize your score in the Class X Social Science examination. The book includes 10 exhaustive sample papers in Social Science developed by experienced teachers at Career Launcher to help you practice in the most efficient manner possible. Moreover, we've included the Solved Paper of 2019 Board Exams so that you familiarize yourself with the exam pattern.

The tests are followed by a detailed marking scheme, which will provide you with clarity on how to go about writing answers, as well as gauge where exactly you stand, in terms of marks obtained.

We hope you enjoy studying this book, as much as we enjoyed creating it.

On behalf of every one of us at Career Launcher, we wish you success in the Board exams, and a glorious career ahead!

Blueprint & Marks Distribution

COURSE STRUCTURE
CLASS X (2016–20)

Theory Paper

Time: 3 Hrs.			Max. Marks : 80
No.	**Units**	**No. of Periods**	**Marks**
I	India and the Contemporary World – II	60	20
II	Contemporary India – II	55	20
III	Democratic Politics – II	50	20
IV	Understanding Economic Development	50	20
	Total	215	80

Unit 1: India and the Contemporary World – II	60 Periods
Themes	**Learning Objectives**
Section 1: Events and Processes: **1. The Rise of Nationalism in Europe:** • The French Revolution and the Idea of the Nation • The Making of Nationalism in Europe • The Age of Revolutions: 1830-1848 • The Making of Germany and Italy • Visualizing the Nation • Nationalism and Imperialism **2. Nationalism in India:** • The First World War, Khilafat and Non - Cooperation • Differing Strands within the Movement • Towards Civil Disobedience • The Sense of Collective Belonging	• Enable the learners to identify and comprehend the forms in which nationalism developed along with the formation of nation states in Europe in the post-1830 period. • Establish the relationship and bring out the difference between European nationalism and anti- colonial nationalisms. • Understand the way the idea of nationalism emerged and led to the formation of nation states in Europe and elsewhere. • Recognize the characteristics of Indian nationalism through a case study of Non-Cooperation and Civil Disobedience Movement. • Analyze the nature of the diverse social movements of the time. • Familiarize with the writings and ideals of different political groups and individuals. • Appreciate the ideas promoting Pan Indian belongingness.

Section 2: Livelihoods, Economies and Societies: Any **one theme** of the following:

3. The Making of a Global World:

- The Pre-modern world
- The Nineteenth Century (1815-1914)
- The Inter war Economy
- Rebuilding a World Economy: The Post-War Era

- Show that globalization has a long history and point to the shifts within the process.
- Analyze the implication of globalization for local economies.
- Discuss how globalization is experienced differently by different social groups.

4. The Age of Industrialization:

- Before the Industrial Revolution
- Hand Labour and Steam Power
- Industrialization in the colonies
- Factories Come Up
- The Peculiarities of Industrial Growth
- Market for Goods

- Familiarize with the Pro- to-Industrial phase and Early – factory system.
- Familiarize with the process of industrialization and its impact on labour class.
- Enable them to understand industrialization in the colonies with reference to Textile industries.

Section 3: Everyday Life, Culture and Politics:

5. Print Culture and the Modern World:

- The First Printed Books
- Print Comes to Europe
- The Print Revolution and its Impact
- The Reading Mania
- The Nineteenth Century
- India and the World of Print
- Religious Reform and Public Debates
- New Forms of Publication
- Print and Censorship

- Identify the link between print culture and the circulation of ideas.
- Familiarize with pictures, cartoons, extracts from propaganda literature and newspaper debates on important events and issues in the past.
- Understand that forms of writing have a specific history, and that they reflect historical changes within society and shape the forces of change.

Unit 2: Contemporary India – II	55 Periods
Themes	**Learning Objectives**
1. Resources and Development: • Types of Resources • Development of Resources • Resource Planning in India • Land Resources • Land Utilization • Land Use Pattern in India • Land Degradation and Conservation Measures • Soil as a Resource • Classification of Soils • Soil Erosion and Soil Conservation	• Understand the value of resources and the need for their judicious utilization and conservation.
2. Forest and Wildlife • Biodiversity or Biological Diversity • Flora and Fauna in India • Vanishing Forests • Asiatic Cheetah: Where did they go? • The Himalayan Yew in trouble • Conservation of forest and wildlife in India • Project Tiger • Types and distribution of forests and wildlife resources • Community and Conservation *Note: The chapter 'Forest and Wildlife' to be assessed in the Periodic Tests only and will not be evaluated in Board Examination.*	• Understand the importance of forests and wild life in one environment as well as develop concept towards depletion of resources.
3. Water Resources: • Water Scarcity and The Need for Water Conservation and Management • Multi-Purpose River Projects and Integrated Water Resources Management • Rainwater Harvesting	• Comprehend the importance of water as a resource as well as develop awareness towards its judicious use and conservation.

<table>
<tr><td>

4. Agriculture:
- Types of farming
- Cropping Pattern
- Major Crops
- Technological and Institutional Reforms
- Impact of Globalization on Agriculture

5. Minerals and Energy Resources
- What is a mineral?
- Mode of occurrence of Minerals
- Ferrons and Non-Ferrons Minerals
- Non-Metallic Minerals
- Rock Minerals
- Conservation of Minerals
- Energy Resources
  - Conventional and Non-Conventional
  - Conservation of Energy Resources

6. Manufacturing Industries:
- Importance of manufacturing
- Contribution of Industry to National Economy
- Industrial Location
- Classification of Industries
- Spatial distribution
  Industrial pollution and environmental degradation
- Control of Environmental Degradation

</td><td>

- Explain the importance of agriculture in national economy.
- Identify various types of farming and discuss the various farming methods; describe the spatial distribution of major crops as well as understand the relationship between rainfall regimes and cropping pattern.
- Explain various government policies for institutional as well as technological reforms since independence.

- Identify different types of minerals and energy resources and places of their availability
- Feel the need for their judicious utilization

- Bring out the importance of industries in the national economy as well as understand the regional disparities which resulted due to concentration of industries in some areas.
- Discuss the need for a planned industrial development and debate over the role of government towards sustainable development.

</td></tr>
</table>

7. Life Lines of National Economy:	
<ul><li>Transport – Roadways, Railways, Pipelines, Waterways, Airways</li><li>Communication</li><li>International Trade</li><li>Tourism as a Trade</li></ul>	<ul><li>Explain the importance of transport and communication in the ever-shrinking world.</li><li>Understand the role of trade and tourism in the economic development of a country.</li></ul>

Unit 3: Democratic Politics – II	**50 Periods**
Themes	**Learning Objectives**
1. Power Sharing:<ul><li>Case Studies of Belgium and Sri Lanka</li><li>Why power sharing is desirable?</li><li>Forms of Power Sharing</li></ul>	<ul><li>Familiarize with the centrality of power sharing in a democracy.</li><li>Understand the working of spatial and social power sharing mechanisms.</li></ul>
2. Federalism:<ul><li>What is Federalism?</li><li>What make India a Federal Country?</li><li>How is Federalism practiced?</li><li>Decentralization in India</li></ul>	<ul><li>Analyse federal provisions and institutions.</li><li>Explain decentralization in rural and urban areas.</li></ul>
3. Democracy and Diversity:<ul><li>Case Studies of Mexico</li><li>Differences, similarities and divisions</li><li>Politics of social divisions</li></ul> *Note: The chapter 'Democracy and Diversity' to be assessed in the Periodic Tests only and will not be evaluated in Board Examination.*	<ul><li>Analyse the relationship between social cleavages and political competition with reference to Indian situation.</li></ul>
4. Gender, Religion and Caste:<ul><li>Gender and Politics</li><li>Religion, Communalism and Politics</li><li>Caste and Politics</li></ul>	<ul><li>Identify and analyse the challenges posed by communalism to Indian democracy.</li><li>Recognise the enabling and disabling effects of caste and ethnicity in politics.</li><li>Develop a gender perspective on politics.</li></ul>

5. Popular Struggles and Movements: • Popular Struggles in Nepal and Bolivia • Mobilization and Organization • Pressure Groups and Movements *Note: The chapter 'Popular Struggles and Movements' to be assessed in the Periodic Tests only and will not be evaluated in Board Examination.*	• Understand the vital role of people's struggle in the expansion of democracy.
6. Political Parties: • Why do we need Political Parties? • How many Parties should we have? • National Political Parties • State Parties • Challenges to Political Parties • How can Parties be reformed?	• Analyse party systems in democracies. • Introduction to major political parties, challenges faced by them and reforms in the country.
7. Outcomes of Democracy: • How do we assess democracy's outcomes? • Accountable, responsive and legitimate government • Economic growth and development • Reduction of inequality and poverty • Accommodation of social diversity • Dignity and freedom of the citizens **8. Challenges to Democracy:** • Thinking about challenges • Thinking about Political Reforms • Redefining democracy *Note: The chapter 'Challenges to Democracy' to be assessed in the Periodic*	• Evaluate the functioning of democracies in comparison to alternative forms of governments. • Understand the causes for continuation of democracy in India. • Distinguish between sources of strengths and weaknesses of Indian democracy. • Reflect on the different kinds of measures possible to deepen democracy. • Promote an active and participatory citizenship.

<table>
<tr><td>Tests only and will not be evaluated in Board Examination.</td><td></td></tr>
<tr><td colspan="2">Unit 4: Understanding Economic Development   50 Periods</td></tr>
<tr><td align="center">Themes</td><td align="center">Objectives</td></tr>
<tr><td>

1. **Development:**
   - What Development Promises - Different people different goals
   - Income and other goals
   - National Development
   - How to compare different countries or states?
   - Income and other criteria
   - Public Facilities
   - Sustainability of development

</td><td>

- Familiarize with concepts of macroeconomics.
- Understand the rationale for overall human development in our country, which includes the rise of income, improvements in health and education rather than income.
- Understand the importance of quality of life and sustainable development.

</td></tr>
<tr><td>

2. **Sectors of the Indian Economy:**
   - Sectors of Economic Activities
   - Comparing the three sectors
   - Primary, Secondary and Tertiary Sectors in India
   - Division of sectors as organized and unorganized
   - Sectors in terms of ownership: Public and Private Sectors

</td><td>

- Identify major employment generating sectors.
- Reason out the government investment in different sectors of economy.

</td></tr>
<tr><td>

3. **Money and Credit:**
   - Money as a medium of exchange
   - Modern forms of money
   - Loan activities of Banks
   - Two different credit situations
   - Terms of credit
   - Formal sector credit in India
   - Self Help Groups for the Poor

</td><td>

- Understand money as an economic concept.
- Understand the role of financial institutions from the point of view of day-to- day life.

</td></tr>
<tr><td>

4. **Globalization and the Indian Economy:**
   - Production across countries
   - Interlinking production across countries

</td><td>

- Explain the working of the Global Economic phenomenon.

</td></tr>
</table>

<ul><li>Foreign Trade and integration of markets</li><li>What is globalization?</li><li>Factors that have enabled Globalisation</li><li>World Trade Organisation</li><li>Impact of Globalization on India</li><li>The Struggle for a fair Globalisation</li></ul> **5. Consumer Rights:** *Note: Chapter 5 'Consumer Rights' to be done as Project Work.*	<ul><li>Gets familiarized with the rights and duties as a consumer; and legal measures available to protect from being exploited in markets.</li></ul>

PROJECT WORK
CLASS X (2019–20)

(05 Periods)   **05 Marks**

1.   Every student has to compulsorily undertake any one project on the following topics:

Consumer Awareness

OR

Social Issues

OR

Sustainable Development

2.   Objective: The overall objective of the project work is to help students gain an insight and pragmatic understanding of the theme and see all the Social Science disciplines from interdisciplinary perspective. It should also help in enhancing the Life Skills of the students.

   Students are expected to apply the Social Science concepts that they have learnt over the years in order to prepare the project report.

   If required, students may go out for collecting data and use different primary and secondary resources to prepare the project. If possible, various forms of art may be integrated in the project work.

3.   The distribution of marks over different aspects relating to Project Work is as follows:

S. No.	Aspects	Marks
a.	Content accuracy, originality and analysis	2
b.	Presentation and creativity	2
c.	Viva Voce	1

4.   The projects carried out by the students in different topics should subsequently be shared among themselves through interactive sessions such as exhibitions, panel discussions, etc.

5. All documents pertaining to assessment under this activity should be meticulously maintained by concerned schools.

6. A Summary Report should be prepared highlighting:

   • objectives realized through individual work and group interactions;

   • calendar of activities;

   • innovative ideas generated in the process ;

   • list of questions asked in viva voce.

7. It is to be noted here by all the teachers and students that the projects and models prepared should be made from eco-friendly products without incurring too much expenditure.

8. The Project Report should be handwritten by the students themselves.

9. Records pertaining to projects (internal assessment) of the students will be maintained for a period of three months from the date of declaration of result for verification at the discretion of Board. Subjudiced cases, if any or those involving RTI / Grievances may however be retained beyond three months.

PRESCRIBED BOOKS:

1. India and the Contemporary World-II (History) - Published by NCERT
2. Contemporary India II (Geography) - Published by NCERT
3. Democratic Politics II (Political Science) - Published by NCERT
4. Understanding Economic Development - Published by NCERT
5. Together Towards a Safer India - Part III, a textbook on Disaster Management - Published by CBSE

Note: Please procure latest reprinted edition (2019) of prescribed NCERT textbooks.

SOCIAL SCIENCE (CODE NO. 087)
QUESTION PAPER DESIGN
CLASS X

Time: 3 Hours 　　　　　　　　　　　　　　　　　　**Max. Marks: 80**

Sr. No.	Typology of Questions	Objective Type (1 mark)	SA (3 marks)	LA (5 marks)	Map Skill	Total Marks	Weightage %
1	**Remembering:**Exhibit memory of previously learned material by recalling facts, terms, basic concepts, and answers.	9	3	1	-	23	29%
2	**Understanding:**Demonstrate understanding of facts and ideas by organizing, comparing, translating, interpreting, giving descriptions, and stating main ideas	4	2	2	-	20	25%
3	**Applying:**Solve problems to new situations by applying acquired knowledge, facts, techniques and rules in a different way.	3	1	2	-	16	20%
4	**Analysing and Evaluating:** Examine and break information into parts by identifying motives or causes. Make inferences and find evidence to support generalizations Present and defend opinions by making judgments about information, validity of ideas, or quality of work based on a set of criteria.	2	1	1	-	10	12%
5	**Creating:**Compile information together in a different way by combining elements in a new pattern or proposing alternative solutions.	2	1		-	5	6.5%
6	**Map Skill**				3+3	6	7.6%
	Total	1x20=20	3x8 =24	5x6=30	6	80	100%

- Internal Assessment: 20 Marks

INTERNAL ASSESSMENT

	Marks	Description	
Periodic Assessment	10 Marks	Pen Paper Test	**5 marks**
		Assessment using multiple strategies For example, Quiz, Debate, Role Play, Viva, Group Discussion, Visual Expression, Interactive Bulletin Boards, Gallery Walks, Exit Cards, Concept Maps, Peer Assessment, Self-Assessment, etc.	**5 marks**
Portfolio	5 Marks	<ul><li>Classwork</li><li>Work done (Activities / Assignments)</li><li>Reflections, Narrations, Journals, etc.</li><li>Achievements of the student in thesubject throughout the year</li><li>Participation of the student in differentactivities like Heritage India Quiz</li></ul>	
Subject Enrichment Activity	5 Marks	<ul><li>Project Work</li></ul>	

LIST OF MAP ITEMS
CLASS X (2019-20)

A. HISTORY (Outline Political Map of India)

Chapter - 3 Nationalism in India – (1918 – 1930) for locating and labelling / Identification

1. Indian National Congress Sessions:

   a. Calcutta (Sep. 1920)

   b. Nagpur (Dec. 1920)

   c. Madras (1927)

2. Important Centres of Indian National Movement

   a. Champaran (Bihar) - Movement of Indigo Planters

   b. Kheda (Gujrat) - Peasant Satyagrah

   c. Ahmedabad (Gujarat) - Cotton Mill Workers Satyagraha

   d. Amritsar (Punjab) - Jallianwala Bagh Incident

   e. Chauri Chaura (U.P.) - Calling off the Non-Cooperation Movement

   f. Dandi (Gujarat) - Civil Disobedience Movement

B. GEOGRAPHY (Outline Political Map of India)

Chapter 1: Resources and Development (Identification only)

   a. Major soil Types

Chapter 3: Water Resources (Locating and Labelling)

Dams:

   a. Salal

   e. Sardar Sarovar

   b. Bhakra Nangal   f. Hirakud

   c. Tehri   g. Nagarjuna Sagar

   d. Rana Pratap Sagar   h. Tungabhadra

Note: The chapter I¥ Water Resources to be assessed in the Periodic Tests only and will not be evaluated in Board Examination.

Chapter 4: Agriculture (Identification only)

a. Major areas of Rice and Wheat

b. Largest / Major producer states of Sugarcane, Tea, Coffee, Rubber, Cotton and Jute

Chapter 5: Minerals and Energy Resources

Minerals (Identification only)

a. Iron Ore mines

- Mayurbhanj
- Durg
- Bailadila
- Bellary
- Kudremukh

b. Coal Mines

- Raniganj
- Bokaro
- Talcher
- Neyveli

c. Oil Fields

- Digboi
- Naharkatia
- Mumbai High
- Bassien
- Kalol
- Ankaleshwar

Power Plants

(Locating and Labelling only)

a. Thermal

- Namrup
- Singrauli
- Ramagundam

b. Nuclear

- Narora
- Kakrapara
- Tarapur
- Kalpakkam

Chapter 6: Manufacturing Industries (Locating and Labelling Only)

Cotton Textile Industries:

a. Mumbai	b. Indore
c. Surat	d. Kanpur
e. Coimbatore	

Iron and Steel Plants:

a. Durgapur	b. Bokaro
c. Jamshedpur	d. Bhilai
e. Vijaynagar	f. Salem

Software Technology Parks:

a. Noida	b. Gandhinagar
c. Mumbai	d. Pune
e. Hyderabad	f. Bengaluru
g. Chennai	h. Thiruvananthapuram

Chapter 7: Lifelines of National Economy

Major Ports: (Locating and Labelling)

a. Kandla	b. Mumbai
c. Marmagao	d. New Mangalore
e. Kochi	f. Tuticorin
g. Chennai	h. Vishakhapatnam
i. Paradip	j. Haldia

International Airports:

a. Amritsar (Raja Sansi)

b. Delhi (Indira Gandhi International)

c. Mumbai (Chhatrapati Shivaji)

d. Chennai (Meenam Bakkam)

e. Kolkata (Netaji Subhash Chandra Bose)

f. Hyderabad (Rajiv Gandhi)

Note:Items of Locating and Labelling may also be given for Identification.

CBSE
Sample Question Paper 1

Social Science
Class X

Time : 3 hrs | **MM : 80**

SECTION A

1. The concept of __________ emerged in Europe during the nineteenth century.   1

2. In Brussels, __________ people are in minority.   1

3. The __________ sector is becoming very important in India.   1

4. Match the following: 1

Column - A	Column - B
Zaid	Source of Protein
Jute	Industrial crop
Rubber	Golden fibre
Pulses	Agricultural season

5. Which religious reformer was responsible for the reformation movement?　1
    (i)   Marco Polo
    (ii) Martin Luther
    (iii) Johann Gutenberg
    (iv) George Elliot

6. What is patriarchy?　1
    (i)   A system where mother is the head of the family
    (ii) A system where there is no head of the family
    (iii) A system where father is the head of the family
    (iv) A system where grandparents have control over family matters

7. Which of these is a regional party of West Bengal?　1
    (i)   Congress
    (ii) DMK
    (iii) AIADMK
    (iv) Trinamool Congress

8. All final goods and services produced during a year make up the:　1
    (i)   National Income
    (ii) State production
    (iii) GST
    (iv) All of the above

9. The most common indicator for measuring economic development of a country is:
    (i)   Average income　1
    (ii) Per Capita income
    (iii) National income
    (iv) Human Development Index

OR

Which of the following neighbouring countries has better performance in terms of human development than India?
    (i)   Bangladesh
    (ii) Nepal
    (iii) Pakistan
    (iv) Sri Lanka

10. Under dictatorship, all the powers are vested in a single person or in a group of people.(True/False)　1

11. Rapid improvement in information and communication technology has slowed down the globalisation process. (True/False)   1

12. The Rowlatt Act was passed by the Imperial Legislative Council in 1919.(True/False)   1

13. Identify the female allegory in the picture above.   1

14. Define Federalism.   1

OR

How many subjects are there in the Union List?

15. What are intermediate goods?   1

16. Who led a peasant movement during the Non-Cooperation Movement?   1

17. What is the meaning of investment?   1

18. When was Rio de Janeiro Earth Summit conducted?   1

19. What are pipelines used for?   1

20. Koderma is the leading producer of which mineral?   1

Section B

21. What were the 'Corn Laws'? Why was it abolished?   3

OR

State any three reasons for the clashes between Gomasthas and weavers.

22. How is the ethnic composition of Belgium very complex? Explain.   3

23. What factors make mineral extractions commercially viable?   3

OR

Describe any three main features of 'Rabi crop'.

24. How can the workers in the unorganized sector be protected?   3

25. Why a democratic government is also called as a legitimate government?   3

OR

Under what conditions can the dignity and freedom of the citizens can be promoted?

26. What is the difference between foreign trade and foreign investment?   3

27. Describe the three-tier system of Indian federation.   3

28. Why is the issue of sustainability important for development?   3

Section C

29. How did Gandhiji convert the National Movement into a Mass Movement?   5

30. What are the characteristics of a political party?   5

OR

The focus on caste in politics can sometimes give an impression that elections are all about caste and nothing else. Do you agree? Explain.

31. What were the provisions of the Treaty of Vienna of 1815?   5

32. The economic strength of a country lies in the development of manufacturing industries. Explain.   5

OR

Explain any two main challenges faced by the jute industry in India. Explain any three objectives of National Jute Policy.

33. "Conservation of minerals is the need of the hour". Support the statement.   5

34. "Poor households still depend on informal sources of credit". Support the statement with examples.   5

Section D

35. (a) Two items A and B are shown in the given political outline map of India. Identify these items with the help of following information and write their correct names on the lines marked on the map.

(A) The place where Jallianwalla Bagh massacre took place.   1

(B) The place where Indian National Congress session was held in 1927.

1

On the same political map, locate and label the following:

(C) The place where Mahatma Gandhi organised Satyagraha Movement in 1918.   1

35. (b) Two items (1) and (2) are shown in the given political outline map of India. Identify these items with the help of following information and write their correct names on the lines marked on the map.

   (1) Iron and steel centre   1

   (2) Major sea port   1

   On the same political map, locate and label the following:

   (3) A Software technology park   1

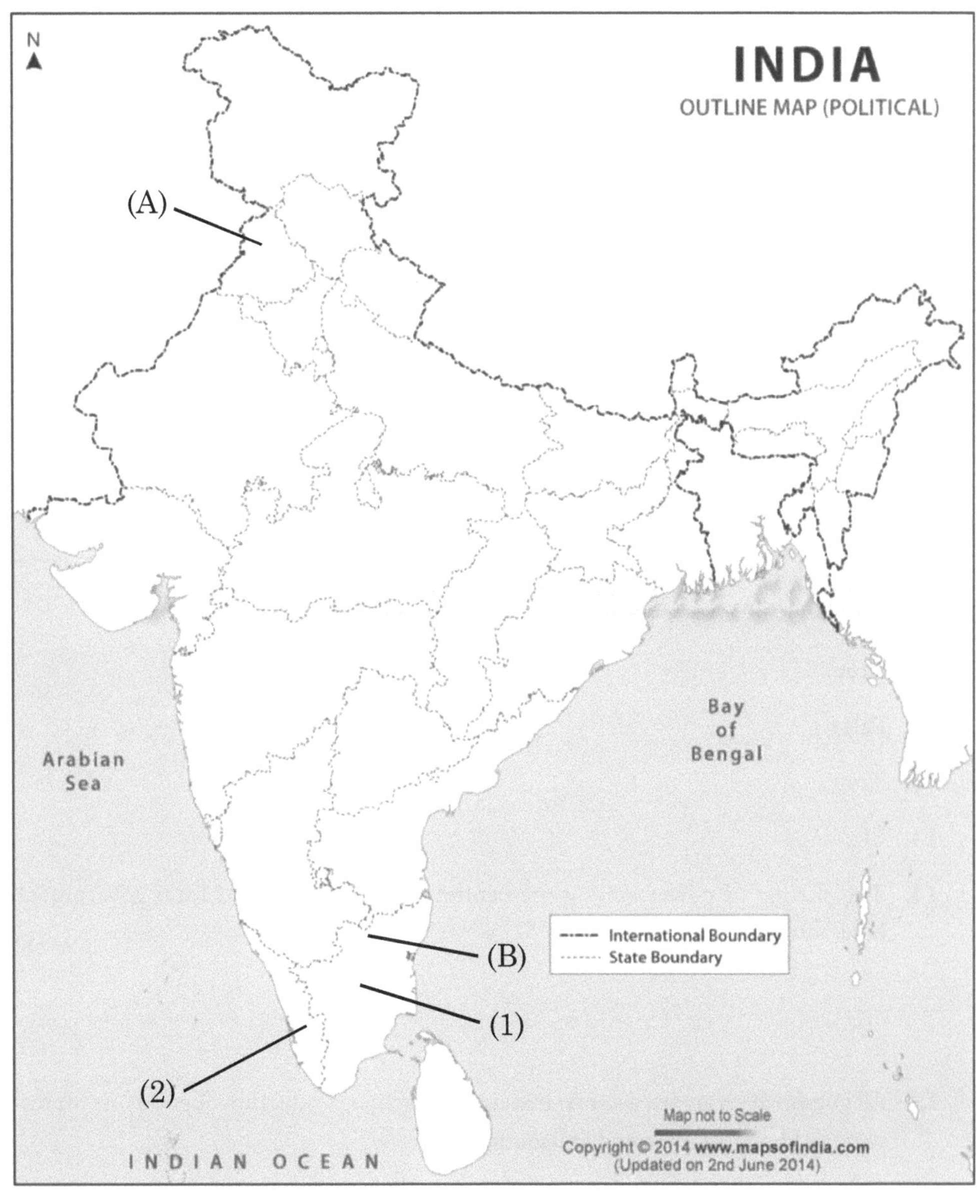

Solution

SECTION A

1. Nationalism　(1)

2. Dutch　(1)

3. Tertiary　(1)

4.

Colum - A	Colum B	(1)
Zaid	Agricultural season	
Jute	Golden fibre	
Rubber	Industrial crop	
Pulses	Source of Protein	

5. (ii) Martin Luther　(1)

6. (iii) A system where father is the head of the family　(1)

7. (iv) Trinamool Congress　(1)

8. (i) National Income　(1)

9. (ii) Per Capita Income　(1)

OR

(iv) Sri Lanka

10. True　(1)

11. False　(1)

12. True　(1)

13. Marianne　(1)

14. The sharing of power among the central, state, regional and local governments is known as federalism.　(1)

OR

97

15. All goods which are used as raw material for further production of goods, or for resale in the same year are known as intermediate goods.　(1)

16. Baba Ramchandra (1)

17. The money that is spent to buy assets such as land, building machines and other equipment is called investment. (1)

18. In June 1992 (1)

19. Pipelines are used for the transportation of crude oil, petroleum products and natural gas. (1)

20. Mica (1)

SECTION B

21. The laws allowing the British Government to restrict the import of corn were known as the "Corn Laws".

These laws were abolished because as industrialists and urban dwellers were unhappy increased food prices; as a result of which they forced the abolition of the Corn Laws. This led to the food being imported into Britain at a much cheaper rate.. Many English farmers left their profession and migrated to towns and cities. $(1 + 2)$

OR

Gomasthas and weavers clashed with each other because of the following reasons:

(a) The gomasthas were outsiders and had no social link with villages.

(b) They were arrogant.

(c) They marched into the villages with sepoys and peons.

(d) They punished weavers for the delays in supply. (Any three) $(1+1+1)$

22. The ethnic composition of Belgium very complex as:

(a) Of the country's total population, 59 per cent live in the Flemish region and speak the Dutch language.

(b) Another 40 per cent of people live in the Wallonia region and speak French.

(c) Remaining 1 per cent of the Belgians speak German.

(d) In the capital city Brussels, 80 percent of people speak French while 20 percent are Dutch speaking. (Any three) $(1 + 1 + 1)$

23. The factors that make mineral extractions commercially viable are:

(a) The minerals content of the ore must be in sufficient concentration.

(b) The type of formation or structure in which they are found determines the relative cases with which mineral ores may be mined.

(c) The mineral should be close to the market so that the transportation cost is low $(1 + 1 + 1)$

OR

Main features of 'Rabi Crop Season':

(a) Rabi crops are sown in Winter from October to December.

(b) Harvested in Summer from April to June.

(c) Important Rabi crops are Wheat, Barley, Peas, Gram and Mustard.

(d) Availability of precipitation during winter months due to western temperate cyclones helps in the success of these crops.   (Any Three)

24. The workers in the unorganized sector be protected in the following ways:

(a) Farmers need to be supported through the adequate facility for timely delivery of seeds, agricultural inputs, credit, storage and marketing outlets.

(b) In urban areas, casual workers need government support for procuring raw material.

(c) Small scale industries also need support for procuring raw material and marketing of the goods. $(1 + 1 + 1)$

25. (i) A democratic government is called a legitimate government because it is people's own government.

(ii) It may be slow, less efficient and not very responsive and clean, but it is people's government.

(iii) There is overwhelming support for the idea of democracy all over the world. People of South Asia, Bangladesh, Sri Lanka, India, Pakistan and Nepal. have no doubt about the suitability of democracy for their own country. $(1 + 1 + 1)$

OR

The conditions are as follows :

(a) To promote the dignity and freedom of the citizens, all individuals should be treated as equal. Once this principle is recognised, it becomes easier for individuals to wage a struggle against what is not acceptable legally and morally.

(b) Claims of the disadvantaged and discriminated for equal status and equal opportunity should be strengthened. Inequalities and atrocities lack moral and legal foundations. $(1.5 + 1.5)$

26. Foreign Trade : The process of buying and selling goods and services between two or more than two countries is known as foreign trade.

Foreign Investment : Foreign investment involves capital flows from one country to another, granting extensive ownership stakes in domestic companies and assets. $(1.5 + 1.5)$

27. Three-tier system means three levels of government. The Indian Constitution was originally provided for a two-tier system of government:

(a) The Union Government or the Central Government.

(b) The State Governments.

(c) But, later a third-tier of federalism was added in the form of Panchayats at the rural level and municipalities at the urban level. Every level enjoys separate jurisdiction $(1 + 1 + 1)$

28. Importance of Sustainable Development :

(a) Sustainable development aims at fulfilling the needs of today without compromising the needs of the future generation.

(b) Sustainability is the capability to use the resources judiciously and maintain ecological balance.

(c) It lays emphasis on environmental protection and checks environmental degradation.

(d) To stop over-exploitation and overuse of resources.   (Any three) $(1 + 1 + 1)$

SECTION C

29. Gandhiji converted the National Movement into a Mass Movement by :

(a) His simple and saintly life and style of convincing the masses made him popular.

(b) His undisputed leadership and magnetic personality.

(c) His policy of non-violent Satyagraha.

(d) His programmes of social reforms like fighting against untouchability.

(e) His commitment to Hindu-Muslim unity. $(1 + 1 + 1 + 1 + 1)$

30. Following are the characteristics of a political party:

(a) A political party has members who agree on some policies and programmes for the society with a view to promote collective good.

(b) It seeks to implement the policies by winning popular support through elections.

(c) A political party has three components: the leaders, the active members and the followers.

(d) A political party is a group of people who come together to contest elections and hold power in the government. $(1\frac{1}{4} \times 4)$

OR

No, I do not agree with this statement.

This is far from true because :

(a) No parliamentary constituency in the country has a clear majority of one single caste. So, every candidate and party needs to win the confidence of more than one caste and community to win elections.

(b) No party wins the votes of all the voters of a caste or community. When people say that a caste is a 'vote bank' of one party, it usually means that a large proportion of the voters from the caste vote for the party.

(c) Many political parties may put up candidates from the same caste (if that caste is believed to dominate the electorate in a particular constituency). Some voters have more than one candidate from their caste while many voters have no candidates from their caste.

(d) The ruling party of the sitting MP or MLA frequently loses elections in our country. That could not have happened if all castes or communities were frozen in their political preferences.

$$(1 + 4)$$

31. Provisions of Treaty of Vienna (1815) :

(a) Bourbon dynasty was restored to power in France.

(b) France lost the territories it had annexed under Napoleon.

(c) The kingdom of Netherlands was set up in the north and Genoa was added to Piedmont in the south.

(d) Prussia was given new territories on its western frontiers.

(e) Austria was given control of northern Italy.

(f) Russia was given a part of Poland and Prussia was given a part of Saxony

$$\text{(Any five)} \ (1 + 1 + 1 + 1 + 1)$$

32. The economic strength of a country lies in the development of manufacturing industries because:

(a) Manufacturing industries help in modernizing agriculture which forms the backbone of our economy.

(b) It reduces the heavy dependence of people on the agriculture sector and creates jobs in secondary and tertiary sectors.

(c) It is necessary for the removal of unemployment and poverty.

(d) It brings down regional disparities.

(e) Export of manufactured goods expands trade and commerce and enhances prosperity.

(f) It brings much needed foreign exchange. $\text{(Any five)} \ (1 + 1 + 1 + 1 + 1)$

OR

The two challenges faced by the jute industry in India are:

(a) Due to its high cost, it is losing market to synthetic fibres and packing materials, particularly the nylon.

(b) India is facing stiff competition from other jute producing nations like Bangladesh, Brazil, Philippines, Egypt and Thailand.

The major objectives of the National Jute Policy, 2005 are :

(a) To increase productivity.

(b) To improve quality.

(c) To ensure good prices to the jute farmers. $(2 + 3)$

33. Conservation of minerals is the need of the hour :

(a) Minerals are considered to be the backbone of the economy.

(b) Industry and agriculture depend on mineral deposits.

(c) The substances manufactured from them also depend on mineral deposits.

(d) Total volume of workable mineral deposits is very less-only 1% of the earth's crust.

(e) Mineral resources are being consumed rapidly, and minerals require millions of years to be created and concentrated.

(f) The geological processes of mineral formation are so slow that the rates of replenishment are infinitely small in comparison to the present rates of consumption.

(g) Minerals resources are finite and non-renewable.

(h) The rich mineral deposits of our country are extremely valuable but short-lived possessions.

(Any five)

34. Poor households still depend on informal sources of credit because :

(a) Banks are not present everywhere in the rural areas.

(b) Even when they are present, getting a loan from the bank is much more difficult than taking a loan from informal sources.

(c) Mega banks or public sector banks require proper documents and collateral.

(d) Absence of collateral is one of the major reasons which prevents the poor from getting bank loans.

(e) Informal lenders such as moneylenders know the borrowers personally and they are willing to give a loan without collateral. $(1 + 1 + 1 + 1 + 1)$

SECTION D $(3+3)$

35. (a) (A) Amritsar

         (B) Nagpur

         (C) Kheda

35. (b) (1) Salem

         (2) Kochi

         (3) Chennai

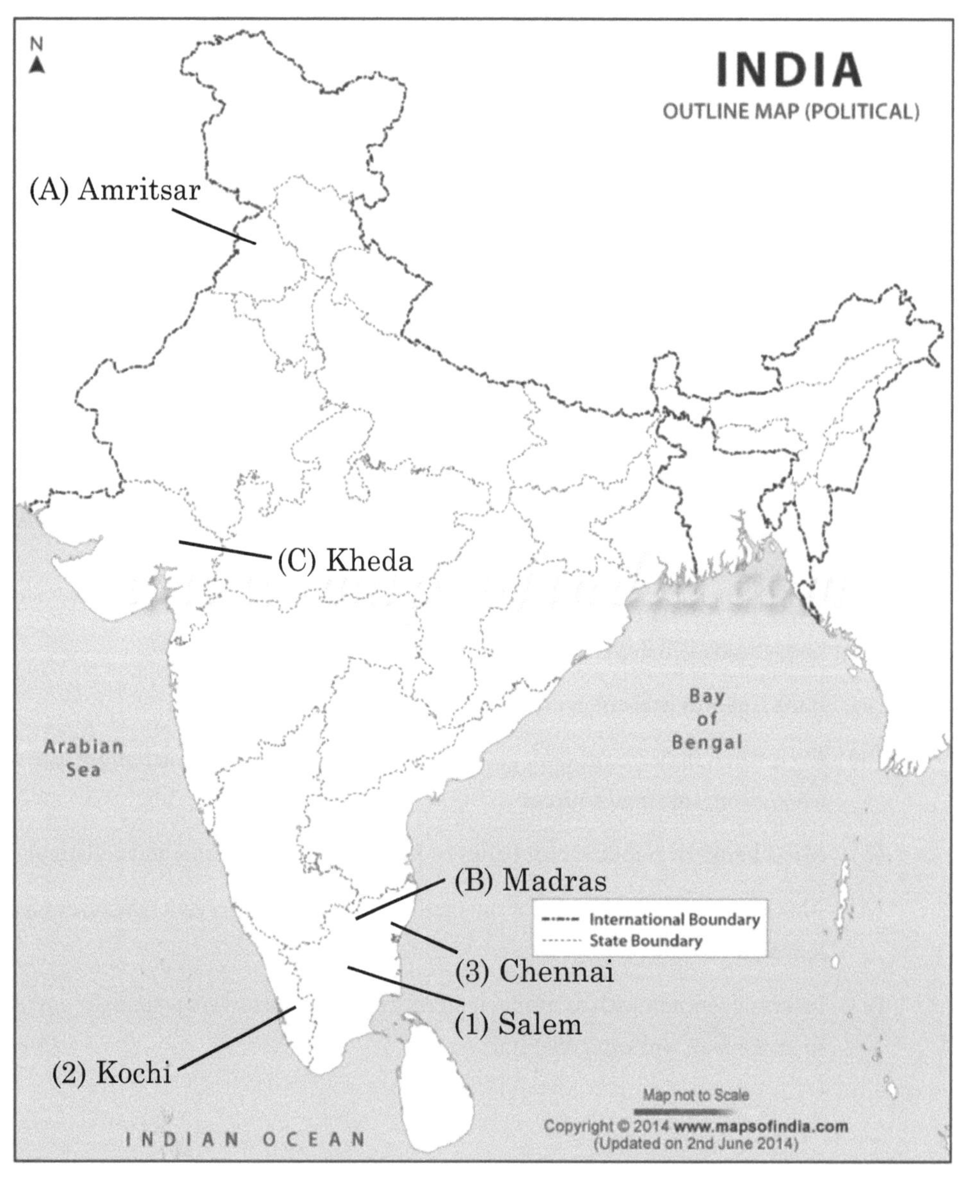

CBSE
Sample Question Paper 2

Social Science
Class X

Time : 3 hrs	MM : 80

SECTION A

1. Napoleon ruled France from: 1

   (i) 1789 to 1815   (ii) 1799 to 1815

   (iii) 1791 to 1815   (iv) 1715 to 1899

2. Why is India a secular state?   1

   (i) Because it is biased towards a particular religion

   (ii) Because people are allowed to follow only certain religions

   (iii) Because communal politics is common in India

   (iv) Because there is no official religion for the Indian state

3. National Rural Employment Guarantee Act was launched in: 1

   (i) 2005   (ii) 2003

   (iii) 2000   (iv) 1995

4. Who implements projects related to Super Highways?   1

    (i) NITI   (ii) NHAI

    (iii) UGC   (iv) MLA

5. Chinese paper reached Europe through the silk route.(True/False)   1

6. Martin Luther wrote Ninety Five Theses.(True/False)   1

7. The Reserve Bank of India cannot issue currency notes and coins on behalf of the central government.(True/False)   1

8. Soil is a natural resource.(True/False)   1

9. Kharif crops require low temperature.(True/False)   1

10. __________ was the principal opposition party in Lok Sabha in 2004.   1

11. Cotton is an example of _________ industry.   1

12. ____________ is a political and socio-economic philosophy that promotes the interests of a nation as a whole.   1

13. Public facilities are provided by the ______________.   1

14. Peasants' Movement in Champaran began in ____________.   1

15. Extraction of valuable minerals or other geological materials from the earth is called _______.   1

16. In which session of the Indian National Congress was the idea of Non-Cooperation Movement accepted?   1

17. When was Sinhala recognised as the official language of Sri Lanka?   1

18. Which organisation aims to liberate international trade?   1

19. Which city is known as electronic capital of India?   1

20. Why was States Reorganisation Commission formed?   1

SECTION B

21. How do MNCs set up production units in other countries?   3

22. Differentiate between horizontal and vertical division of powers.   3

23. Explain any three advantages of globalisation.   3

24. What are the basis of communalism?   3

25. Why were Europeans attracted to the land of Africa?   3

OR

What is meant by proto-industrialisation? Why was it successful in the countryside in England in the 17th Century?

26. How does agriculture gives boost to the industrial sector? 3

27. What are 'placer deposits'? Give examples of minerals found in such deposits. 3

28. What steps were taken by French revolutionaries to create a sense of collective identity among the French people? 3

OR

Write short notes to show what you know about 'The Gutenberg Press'.

Section C

29. Differentiate between formal sector credit and informal sector credit. 5

OR

What is the role of banks in India?

30. Why did Gandhiji decide to launch a nationwide Satyagraha against the proposed Rowlatt Act of 1919? How was it organised? Explain. 5

31. Distinguish between Red soil and laterite soil. 5

32. Why is the tertiary sector growing so rapidly in India? 5

OR

Why is money transaction system better than barter system? Explain with examples.

33. Differentiate between 'Coming Together Federation' and 'Holding Together Federation', with examples. 5

34. What are the various challenges faced by political parties? 5

Section D

35. (a) Two items A and B are shown in the given political outline map of India. Identify these items with the help of following information and write their correct names on the lines marked on the map.

(A) The place where Cotton Mill Workers Satyagraha took place. 1

(B) The place where Indian National Congress session was held in September1920. 1

On the same political map, locate and label the following:

(C) The place where Mahatma Gandhi organised Movement of Indigo Planters. 1

35. (b) Two items (1) and (2) are shown in the given political outline map of India. Identify these items with the help of following information and write their correct names on the lines marked on the map.

(1) An iron ore Mine   1

(2) An oil field   1

On the same political map, locate and label the following:

(3) Narora   1

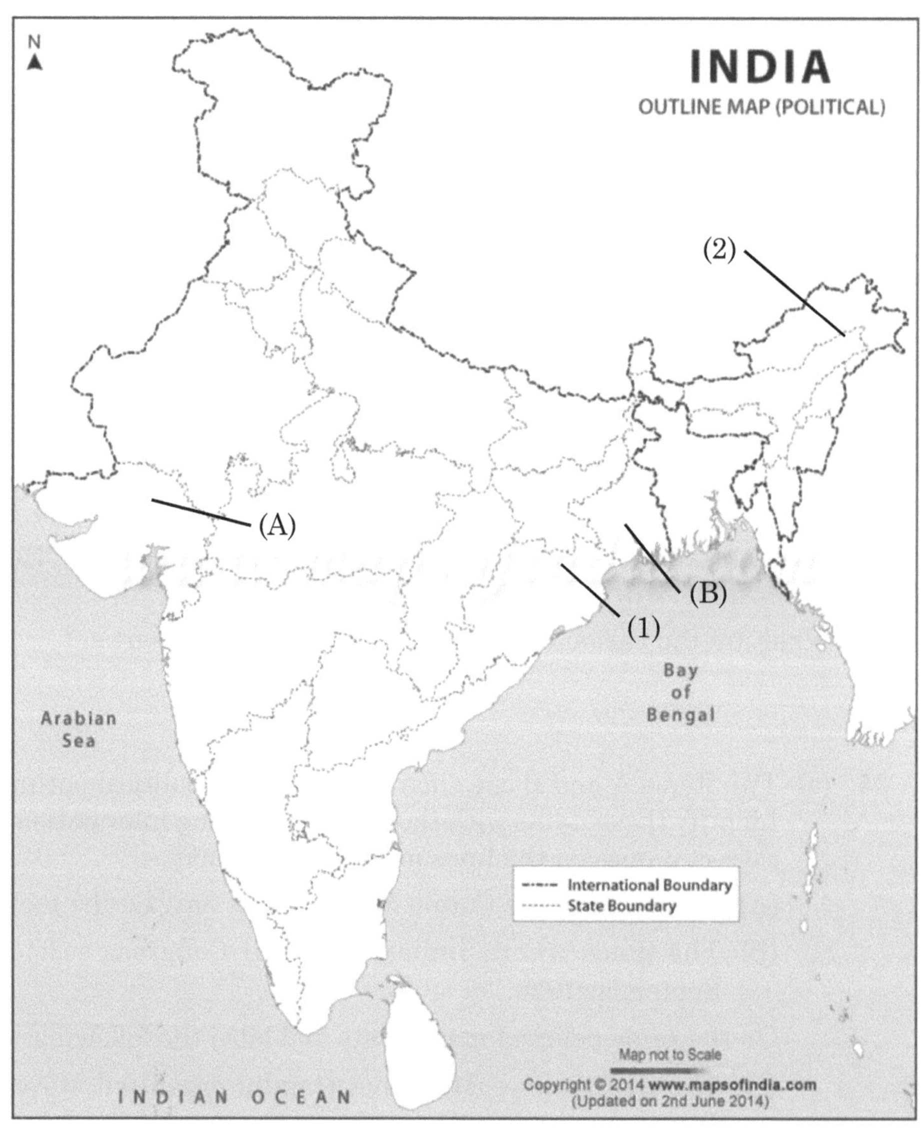

Solution

SECTION A

1. (ii) 1799 to 1815	(1)
2. (iv) Because there is no official religion for the Indian state	(1)
3. (i) 2005	(1)
4. (ii) NHAI	(1)
5. True	(1)
6. True	(1)
7. False	(1)
8. True	(1)
9. False	(1)
10. Bharatiya Janata Party	(1)
11. Agro - Based	(1)
12. Nationalism	(1)
13. Provided by the government	(1)
14. 1916	(1)
15. Mining	(1)
16. Calcutta Session	(1)
17. 1956.	(1)
18. World Trade Organisation	(1)
19. Bengaluru	(1)
20. To recommend creation of states on the linguistic basis	(1)

SECTION B

21. MNCs set up production units in the following ways:

(i)   They work jointly or in partnership with some local companies of the existing country.

(ii) Buy the local companies and then expand its production with the help of modern technology.

(iii) They place orders for small producers and sell these products under their own brand name to the customers worldwide. $(1 + 1 + 1)$

22.

Horizontal	Vertical
1. In this power is shared between legislature, executive and Judiciary.	1. In this power is shared between union, state and local government. (1)
2. It specifies the concept of checks and balances in order to check unlimited powers of the organs.	2. There is no concept of check and balances because powers are given by the constitution from the higher to the lower level. (1)
3. It ensures the concept of the expansion of democracy	3. It promotes the concept of deepening of democracy. (1)

23. • Rapid improvement in technology, especially in the development of information and communication technology (1)

  • Competition among the producers is an advantage to the consumers. (1)

  • It has also created new opportunities for companies producing services, especially in information technology, data entry and accounting. (1)

24. • The followers of a particular religion must belong to one community. (1)

  • It follows that people who follow different religions cannot belong to the same community. (1)

  • It believes that people belonging to different religions cannot live as equal citizens. (1)

25. Europeans were attracted to the land of Africa due to the following reasons:

(i)   The resources of land and minerals of Africa

(ii) To establish plantations and exploit mines.

(iii) African countries were militarily weak and backward. So, it was easy to conquer them.

$$(1 + 1 + 1)$$

OR

Proto-industrialisation is the phase of industrialisation that was not based on the factory system. Before the coming of factories, there was large-scale industrial production for an international market. This part of industrial history is known as proto-industrialisation.

It was successful in the countryside in England due to the following reasons :

(i)   The peasants had been shut out of village commons due to enclosure movement.

(ii) They now looked for the alternative source of income.

26. Agriculture gives boost to the industrial sector in the following ways:

(a)   It provides market for industrial products

(b)   It provides raw material to industries

(c)   It helps boost new industrial products. The industries such as cotton, jute, silk, woolen textiles, sugar and edible oil, etc., are based on agricultural raw materials. $(1 + 1 + 1)$

27. Certain minerals may occur as alluvial deposits in sands of valley floors and base of hills. These deposits are called 'placer deposits'. They generally contain minerals which are not corroded by water.

Gold, silver, tin and platinum are examples of some important minerals found in 'placer deposits'.

$(2+1)$

28. The French revolutionaries took many important steps to create a sense of collective identity among the French people which were:

(a) Ideas of la patrie (the fatherland) and le citoyen (the citizen) emphasising the notion of a united community enjoying equal rights under a constitution.

(b) A new French flag, a tricolour replaced the royal standard.

(c) The Estates General was renamed the National Assembly and was elected by a group of active citizens.

(d) New hymns, oaths and martyrs commemorated in the name of the nation.

(e) A central administrative system made uniform laws for the entire nation.

(f) Discouraging regional dialects and promoting French as a common language of the nation.

$(\frac{1}{2} \times 6)$

OR

From his childhood, Gutenberg had seen wine and olive presses. He had also learnt the art of polishing stones, became a master goldsmith, and acquired the expertise to create lead moulds used for making trinkets. Drawing on this knowledge, Gutenberg adapted existing technology to design his innovation. The olive press provided the model for the printing press, and moulds were used for casting the metal types for the letters of the alphabet.

The first book printed by him was the Bible. About 180 copies were printed and it took three years to produce them. By the standards of time this was fast production. (3)

SECTION C

29.

Formal Sector	Informal Sector	
• Credit is provided by banks and co-operative societies	• Credit is provided by traders and money- Lenders.	(2)
• R.B.I supervises the sector	• No supervision	(1)
• Proper terms of credit like documentation, rate of interest, collateral are followed	• Terms of credit are flexible	(1)
• Rate of interest is low	• Rate of interest is high	(1)

OR

- Provides loans
- Money in safe custody
- Wave loans of the farmers
- Gives interest on savings
- Mediate between people who have surplus and those who need money.

30. Satyagraha against the proposed Rowlatt Act, 1919 :

(a) The Rowlatt Act was hurriedly passed through the Imperial Legislative Council.

(b) Indian members unitedly opposed it.

(c) It gave government enormous powers to repress political activities.

(d) It allowed detention of political prisoners without trials for two years.   (Any two)

Organisation of Satyagraha :

(a) Mahatma Gandhi wanted non-violent civil disobedience against such unjust laws.

(b) It was started with a 'Hartal' on 6th April.

(c) Rallies were organised in various cities.

(d) Workers went on strike in railway workshops.

(e) Shops were closed down.   (Any three) 2 + 3 = 5

31.

Red soil	Laterite soil	
• It is formed due to weathering of igneous and metamorphic rocks	• It is formed by leaching process in the tropical areas.	(1)
• Highly porous and less fertile but when deep, it is fertile.	• It is less fertile	(1)
• less crystalline	• Crystalline	(1)
• red in colour due to iron	• red in color due to little clay and much gravel of red sandstone	(1)
• found in Tamil Nadu, Karnataka Andhra, Orissa and Jharkhand	• found in the hills of Deccan, Kerala, Orissa, Assam and Meghalaya.	(1)

32. Tertiary sector is growing in India so rapidly because:-

(a) In any country several services such as hospitals, educational institutions, post and telegraph services, Police Stations, courts, villages administrative offices, Municipal Corporation, defence, transport, bank, insurance companies, etc. are required. In the developing country the government has take responsibility.

(b) The development of agriculture and industry leads to the development of services such as transport, trade, storage, and the like svf already seen. Greater the development of the primary and secondary sector more would be the demand for such services.

(c) As income level rise, certain sections of people start demanding many more services like eating out, tourism, shopping, private hospitals, private schools, professional training, etc.

(d) Over the past decade or so, certain new services such as those based on Information and Communication Technology have been important and essential. The production of these services has been rising rapidly.

(e) Not all the services sector is growing equally well. Service sector in India employs many different kinds of people. at one end there are limited numbers of services that employee highly skilled and education educated workers. $(1 + 1 + 1 + 1 + 1)$

OR

(i) Transaction system is better than a barter system because the double coincidence of wants creates a problem.

(ii) For example, a shoe manufacturer wants to sell shoes in the market and wants to buy wheat. For this, he would look for a wheat growing farmer who would exchange his wheat with the shoes.

(iii) In a barter system, goods are exchanged without the use of money.

(iv) In contrast, in an economy where money is in use; money provides the crucial intermediate step. $(1\tfrac{1}{4} \times 4 = 5)$

33. Difference between 'Coming Together Federation' and 'Holding Together Federation':

(i) Coming Together Federations are formed when independent states come together to form a bigger state and 'Holding Together Federations' are formed when a large country decides to divide itself into sub-units.

(ii) In 'Coming Together Federations' the state governments are strong, whereas in 'Holding Together Federations', the central government is strong.

(iii) In 'Coming Together Federations', all states governments have equal powers but in 'Holding Together Federations, this may not be the case.

(iv) Examples of Coming Together Federations-the USA, Switzerland and Australia.

Examples of Holding Together Federations - India, Spain and Belgium. $(1 + 4)$

34. (1) *Lack of internal democracy* - As parties do not hold organizational meetings and do not conduct regular internal elections   (2)

(2) *Dynastic succession* - The top post are always controlled by members of our family   (1)

(3) *Money and muscle power* - parties support criminals who raise money and have muscle power   (1)

(4) *Absence of meaningful choice* - There is not much ideological difference between political parties so voters never get any positive option.   (1)

Section D

35. (a)   (A)   Ahmedabad   (3 + 3)

          (B)   Calcutta

          (C)   Champaran

35. (b)   (1)   Mayurbhanj

          (2)   Digboi

          (3)   Narora

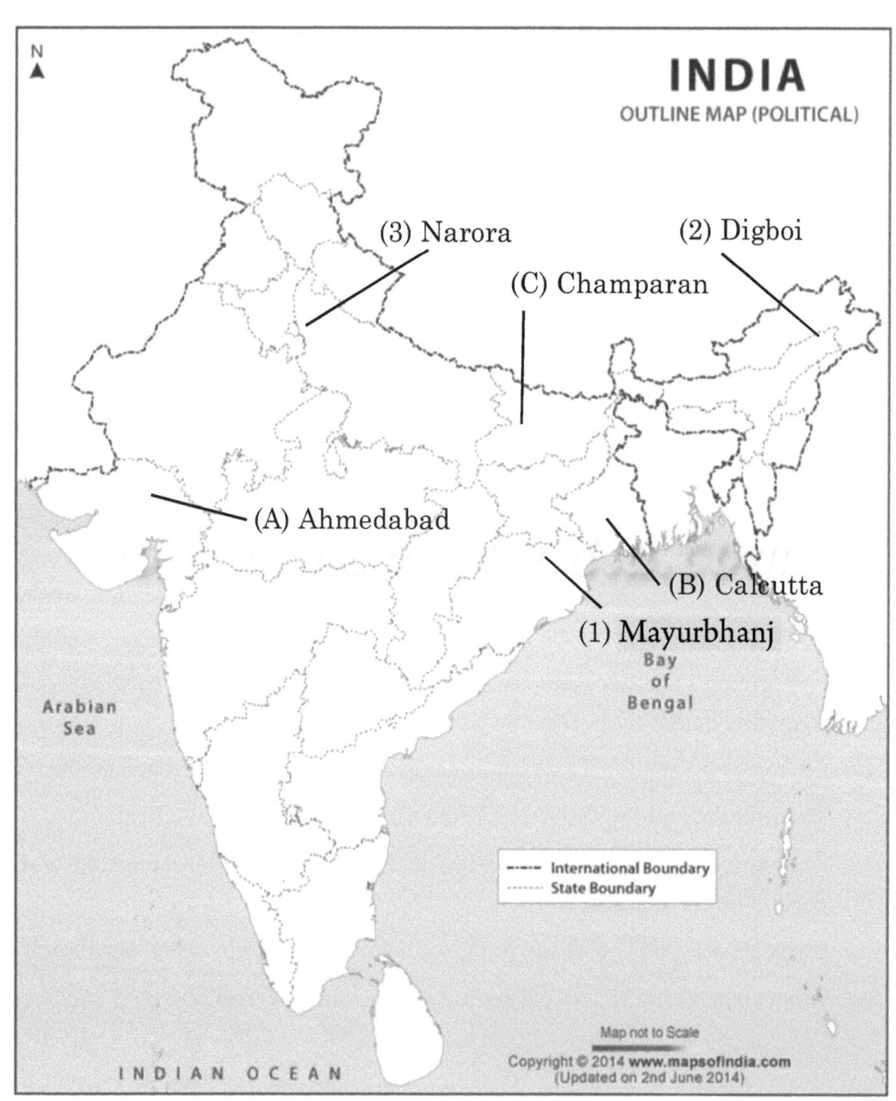

CBSE
Sample Question Paper 3

Social Science
Class X

Time : 3 hrs **MM : 80**

General Instructions

i. The question paper has **35** questions in all.
ii. Marks are indicated against each question.
iii. Questions from serial number **1** to **20** are objective type questions. Each question carries **one mark**. Answer them as instructed.
iv. Questions from serial number **21** to **28** are **3 marks** questions. Answer of these questions should not exceed **80 words** each.
v. Questions from serial number **29** to **34** are **5 marks** questions. Answer of these questions should not exceed **120 words** each.
vi. Question number **35** is a map question of **6 marks** with two parts - **35 a.** from History (3 marks) and **35 b.** from Geography (3 marks).

SECTION A

1. Why did the wheat price fall down by 50 per cent between 1928 and 1934?   1

   (i) Due to less production

   (ii) Due to floods

   (iii) Due to the Great Depression

   (iv) Due to droughts

2. Which city is known as the Manchester of India?   1

   (i) Chennai   (ii) Jaipur

   (iii) Delhi   (iv) Mumbai

3. Which of the following industries use bauxite as a raw material?   1

   (i) Cotton   (ii) Aluminum

   (iii) Steel   (iv) Jute

4. In ancient India palm leaves was used for writing manuscripts.   1

5. The first International Earth Summit was held in Geneva.   1

6. A democratic form of government is considered the best.   1

7. 146 countries are the members of the WTO.   1

8. The first image of Bharat Mata painted was painted by ____________.   1

9. ____________ river is declared as National Waterway No. 1.   1

10. Zollverin started in the year ____________ in Prussia.   1

11. The average income is also called as ________________.   1

12. What was the impact of white revolution?   1

13. What was the most important aspect of the Treaty of Constantinople?   1

14. In India, which sector witnesses' maximum labour?   1

15. 'Marriage' as a subject falls under which list?   1

16. Why were workers in England hostile to machines and new technology?   1

17. "There is enough for everybody's need but not for anybody's greed "Who said this?   1

OR

Which cold desert is relatively isolated from the rest of the country?

18. State the meaning of underemployment.   1

19. What is main objective of the Feminist Movement?   1

20. How can you say that democracies are based on political equality?   1

Section B

21. What is meant by the term "resource"? List the types of resources classified on the basis of its ownership.   3

22. What is meant by economic development? What are the two bases of measuring economic development of a country?   3

23. State the effects of the British Government's decision for the abolition of the Corn Laws.   3

OR

Why did women workers in Britain attack the Spinning Jenny?

24. How is communalism a hindrance in the functioning of our democracy?   3

25. How is the concept of Self-Help Groups important for poor people?   3

26. Which are the two main cropping seasons in India? Mention their growing and harvesting periods. 3

27. How did the printers manage to attract the people, largely illiterate, towards printed books? 3

28. When is democracy considered successful? 3

Section C

29. Discuss the events of the civil disobedience movement. 5

OR

Why did the Muslims not join the Civil Disobedience Movement?

30. The credit activities of the informal sector should be discouraged – Discuss. 5

OR

What is the role of manufacturing sector in India?

31. Differentiate between National and regional parties. 5

32. What is soil erosion? Suggest measures of soil conservation in hilly, mountainous and in desert areas. 5

33. Define tertiary sector. Describe about the different kinds of people employed in this sector in India. 5

34. What are the advantages of decentralization? 5

Section D

35. (a) Two items A and B are shown in the given political outline map of India. Identify these items with the help of following information and write their correct names on the lines marked on the map.

(A) The place where Indian National Congress session was held in 1927. 1

(B) The place where Civil Disobedience Movement started 1

On the same political map, locate and label the following:

(C) Chauri Chaura 1

35. (b) Two items (1) and (2) are shown in the given political outline map of India. Identify these items with the help of following information and write their correct names on the lines marked on the map.

    (1) A coal mine   1

    (2) An international airport   1

On the same political map, locate and label the following:

    (3) Noida   1

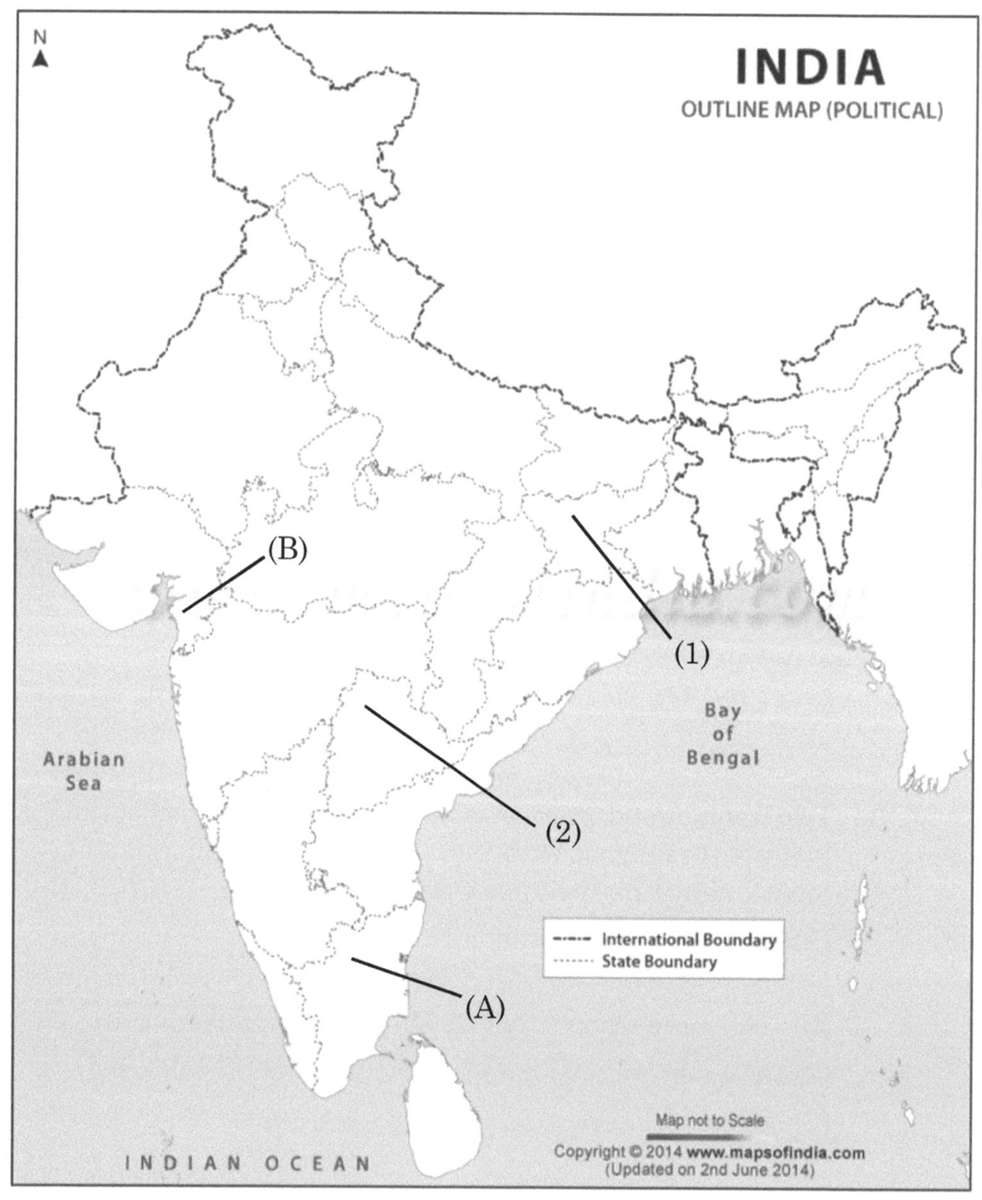

Solution

SECTION A

1. (iii) Due to the Great Depression (1)

2. (iv) Mumbai (1)

3. (ii) Aluminum (1)

4. True (1)

5. False (1)

6. True (1)

7. False (1)

8. Abanindranath Tagore (1)

9. Ganga (1)

10. 1834 (1)

11. Per Capita income (1)

12. increased production of milk (1)

13. recognized Greece as an independent nation (1)

14. Agriculture (1)

15. Concurrent List (1)

16. They feared that they would lose their jobs and livelihood. (1)

17. Mahatma Gandhi (1)

OR

Ladakh

18. People are working less than what they are capable of doing. (1)

19. The main objective of the Feminist Movement is to attain equality among men and women.

(1)

20. Democracy gives political equality by granting every individual the right to vote. (1)

Section B

21. Everything available in our environment, which can be used to satisfy our needs, provided, it is technologically accessible, economically feasible and culturally acceptable, is known as a resource. (1)

    Types of resources on the basis of ownership are:

    (a) Individual resources

    (b) Community resources

    (c) National and international (Any two) (1 + 1)

22. Economic development refers to the adoption of new technologies, transition from agriculture based to industry-based economy and improvement in lifestyle.

    Two bases of measuring development of a country are:

    (a) Average or per capita income.

    (b) National income and public facilities. (1 + 2)

23. (a) Food could be imported into Britain at much cheaper rate than it would be produced within the country.

    (b) British agriculture was unable to compete with imports. Vast areas of land were left uncultivated and people started migrating to cities or other countries.

    (c) As food prices fell, consumption in Britain rose. Faster industrial growth in Britain also led to higher incomes and therefore more food imports. (1 + 1 + 1)

OR

The women workers attacked Spinning Jenny because of the following reasons:

(a) The Spinning Jenny speeded up the spinning process and reduced labour demands.

(b) Many workers were left without any job and became unemployed.

(c) By the use of this machine, a single worker could make a number of spindles and spin several threads. (1 + 1 + 1)

24. Communalism is a hindrance in the functioning of our democracy as:

    (a) Communalism leads to the belief that people belonging to different religions cannot live as equal citizens within one nation. Either, one of them has to dominate the rest or they have to form different nations.

    (b) Any attempt to bring all followers of one religion together in a context other than religion is bound to suppress many voices within that community. (1.5 + 1.5)

25. • They help the borrowers to overcome the problem of lack of collateral.

    • They help them to become financially self reliant.

    • They provide a platform to hold meetings to discuss their problems. (1 + 1 + 1)

26. The two main cropping seasons are Rabi and Kharif.:

(i) Rabi crops are sown in winter from October to December and harvested in summer from April to June.

(ii) Kharif crops are sown with the onset of monsoon in different parts of the country and harvested in September-October. $(1 + 2)$

27. (a) To attract people, the printers started printing popular ballads and folk tales.

(b) To attract people books had been incorporated with lots of illustrations.

(c) Ballads and folk tales were sung and recited to the people in gatherings in the villages.

$(1 + 1 + 1)$

28. Democracy is considered to be successful when:-

(i) The rulers elected by the people take all major decisions and not the rich and powerful.

(ii) The elections offer a free choice and opportunity to the people.

(iii) The choice available to all the people is based on political equality. $(1 \times 3 = 3)$

SECTION C

29. • It began with Gandhi breaking the salt law at Dandi.

• There was boycott of foreign cloth and picketing of liquor shops.

• Forest people violated forest laws.

• Peasants refused to pay revenue and Chaukidari taxes. $(1 + 1 + 2 + 1)$

OR

• Failure of non-co-operation Khilafat movement

• Association of the Congress with Hindu Mahasabha

• Communal clashes

• Muslim leaders concerned about minority status

• Disappointment about end of coil disobedience movement.

30. • No organization to supervise so they charge exorbitant rate of interest.

• They indulge in exploitative practices.

• In certain cases, the amount to be repaid is greater than the income of the borrower.

• Those who wish to start an enterprise may not because of high cost of borrowing.

$(1 + 1 + 1 + 2)$

OR

• Provides large scale employment

• Helps in earning huge revenue

- Helps in the development of nation
- Is responsible for manufacturing
- Helps in the development of primary sector

31.

National Parties	Regional Parties
• They have influence all over the country.	• Influence is limited to a particular area.
• They give priority to the national problems.	• They have more interest in local problems.
• It has atleast 6% votes in Lok Sabha or Assembly election in four states.	• A party has to secure atleast 6% votes in legislative election and win atleast two seats.
• *Examples* – B.J.P/Congress.	• *Examples* – Janta Dal/Akali Dal.

$$(1 + 1 + 2 + 1)$$

32. The denudation or destruction of the soil cover and their subsequent natural removal is termed soil erosion. (2)

The measures to control soil erosion are –

- Contour ploughing can decelerate flow of water down the slopes.
- Terrace cultivation checks downhill flow of water and controls soil erosion.
- Afforestation can help in soil conservation in hilly areas. $(1 + 1 + 1)$

33. Tertiary Sector : It helps in the development of the primary and secondary sectors. They provide aid or support for the production process.

Different kinds of people employed in this sector because it provides lots of opportunity for job.

(i) On one end, there are a limited number of services that employ highly skilled and educated workers.

(ii) On the other end, there are a very large number of workers engaged in services such as small shopkeepers, repair persons, transporters, etc. $(2 + 1\frac{1}{2} + 1\frac{1}{2})$

34. Advantages of Decentralisation :

(i) Sharing of power between centre and states and local government reduces conflicts.

(ii) Large number of problems and issues can be best settled at the local level. People have better knowledge of problems in their localities.

(iii) People have better knowledge of their own problems.

(iv) They know better on where to spend money and how to manage things efficiently.

(v) People at the local level will participate directly in decision making.

$$(1 \times 5 = 5)$$

Section D

35.	(a)	(A) Ahmedabad	(3 + 3)
		(B) Calcutta	
		(C) Champaran	
35.	(b)	(1) Bokaro	
		(2) Digboi	
		(3) Noida	

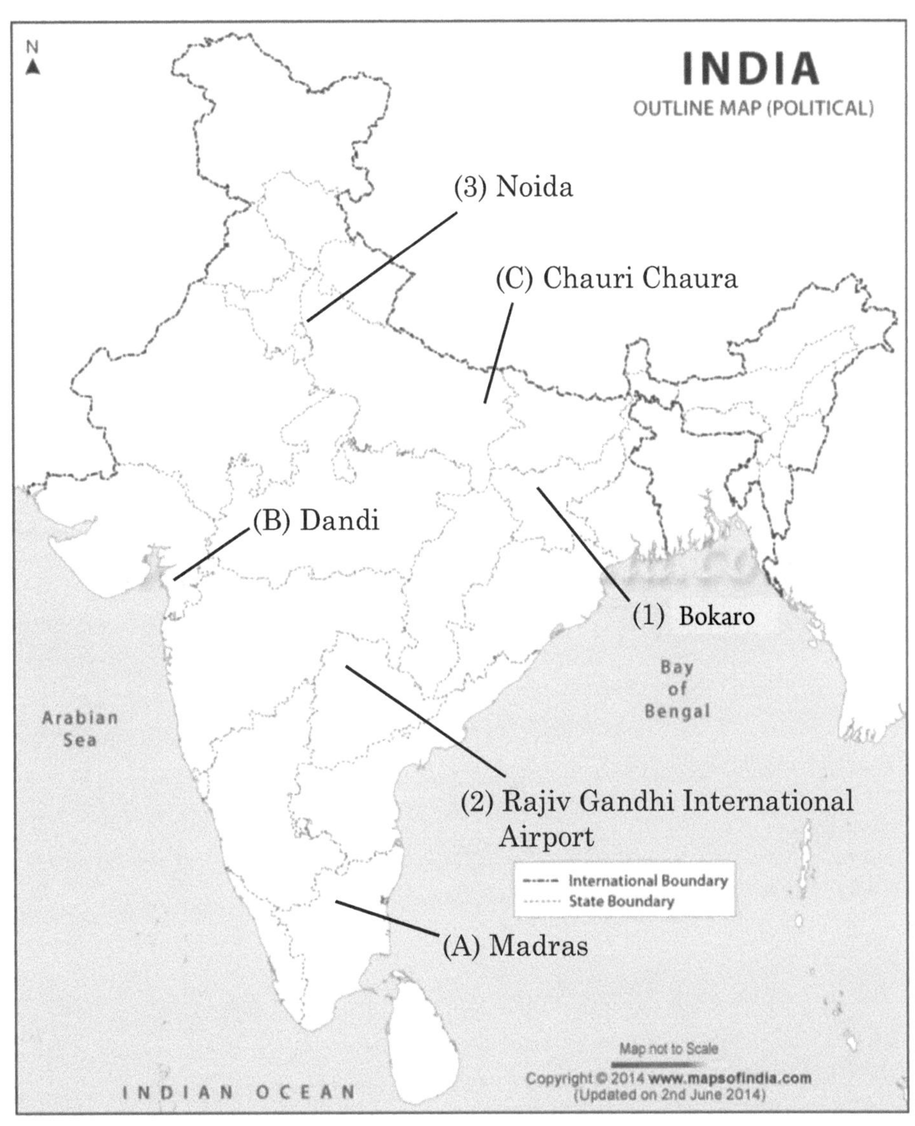

CBSE
Sample Question Paper 4

Social Science
Class X

<table>
<tr><td>Time : 3 hrs</td><td>MM : 80</td></tr>
</table>

SECTION A

1. At which of the following places was the Frankfurt Assembly convened?　　1

   (i) At the church of St. Paul

   (ii) At the church of St. Peters

   (iii) At the palace of Prussia

   (iv) At the Hall of Mirrors in the palace of Versailles

2. In which one of the following states is terrace cultivation practiced?　　1

   (i) Punjab　　　　　　(ii) Plains of Uttar Pradesh

   (iii) Haryana　　　　　(iv) Uttarakhand

3. Why is power sharing good for democracies?   1
   (i)   It gives absolute power to the government.
   (ii) It gives absolute power to the citizens.
   (iii) It reduces the possibility of conflict between social groups.
   (iv) It ensures foreign investments.

4. Which one of the following states has the lowest road density?   1
   (i)   Jammu & Kashmir   (ii) Rajasthan
   (iii) Madhya Pradesh   (iv) Bihar

5. Gully and sheet erosion help in replenishing soil fertility.   1

6. Shaukat Ali and Muhammad Ali led the Khilafat Movement.   1

7. Human development is not the ultimate goal of all economic activities.   1

8. Specialized cultivation of fruits and vegetables is known as Horticulture   1

9. The monazite sands of Kerala are rich in Thorium.   1

10. The emergence of ___________ parties led to the era of coalition governments. 1

11. The activities in primary, secondary and tertiary sectors are ___________.   1

12. The first spinning and weaving mill set up in 1874 at ________________.   1

13. What term is used for a person who thinks that caste is the principal basis of a
    community?   1

14. What was Diamond Sutra?   1

15. What was the problem with Barter system?   1

16. What did the idea of Satyagraha emphasize upon?   1

17. What attracts the foreign investment?   1

18. Which method of hand-printing was developed in China?   1

19. Name two most important sugar producing states of India.   1

20. What is meant by economic inequality?   1

SECTION B

21. Why does the Indian Government gives holidays for the festivals of most of the
    religions."?   3

22. What are border roads? Why are they important?   3

23. What is money? Why is modern money currency accepted as a medium of
    exchange?   3

24. List any three features of the Civil Code of 1804 usually known as the Napoleonic
    Code.   3

25. What are the uses of oilseeds? Which state is the largest producer of groundnut
    in India?   3

26. How can government play a major role in making globalization fair?   3

27. Explain the three types of flows within international economy in exchanges.

3

OR

Why did technological changes occur slowly in Britain in the early nineteenth century?

28. What is the relationship between democracy and development?   3

OR

What are the various challenges faced by political parties?

Section C

29. How much land is degraded at present in India? Explain any four human activities which are responsible for it?   5

30. State the various functions political parties perform in a democracy.   5

31. Why did Gandhiji decide to launch a nationwide 'Satyagraha' against the proposed Rowlatt Act (1919) ? How was it opposed? Explain.   5

OR

Describe the impact of the print revolution in Europe during 15th and 16th century.

32. What are the various sources of credit in rural areas? Which one of them is most popular and why?   5

OR

Why should the credit activities of informal sector discouraged?

33. How did Majoritarianism increase the feeling of alienation among the Sri Lankan Tamils? Explain.   5

34. What is the signific ance of secondary sector in Indian economy? How does it help in the economic development of the country?   5

Section D

35. (a) Two items A and B are shown in the given political outline map of India. Identify these items with the help of following information and write their correct names on the lines marked on the map.

   (A) The place where Non Cooperation movement was called off.   1

   (B) The place where Jallianwalan Bagh massacre took place   1

   On the same political map, locate and label the following:

   (C) The place where Congress session was held in 1920   1

35. (b) Two items (1) and (2) are shown in the given political outline map of India. Identify these items with the help of following information and write their correct names on the lines marked on the map.

(1) An coal mine   1

(2) A thermal power station   1

On the same political map, locate and label the following:

(3) Vijayanagara   1

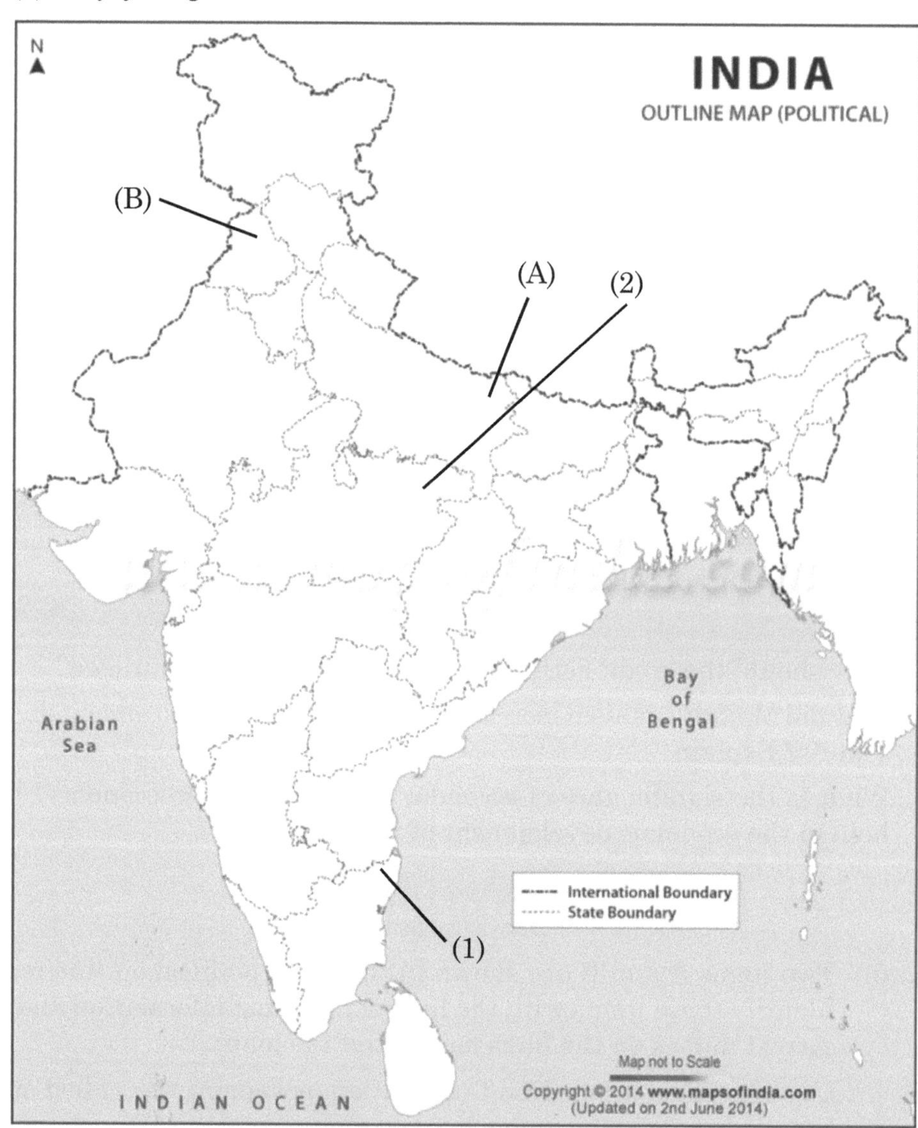

Solution

SECTION A

1. (i) At the church of St. Paul (1)

2. (iv) Uttarakhand (1)

3. (iii) It reduces the possibility of conflict between social groups. (1)

4. (i) Jammu & Kashmir (1)

5. False (1)

6. True (1)

7. False (1)

8. True (1)

9. True (1)

10. Regional parties (1)

11. interdependent (1)

12. Madras (1)

13. Communist (1)

14. The oldest Japanese printed book (1)

15. Problem of double coincidence (1)

16. The power of truth (1)

17. Infrastructural facilities. (1)

18. Woodblock printing (1)

19. Uttar Pradesh and Mararashtra (1)

20. It is the unequal distribution of income and opportunity between different groups in society. (1)

SECTION B

21. The Government of India gives holidays for the festivals of most of the religions because of the following reasons:

    (a) India is a secular state and therefore it does not have any official religion.

    (b) The Constitution provides freedom to all to profess, practice and propagate any religion

    (c) The Constitution prohibits discrimination on the ground of religion. (1 + 1 + 1)

22. Roads in the bordering areas of the country. (1)

Importance

- They have improved accessibility in areas of difficult terrain.

- They Supply military equipments to the borders of our country. (1 + 1)

23. Money is anything that has common acceptability as a means of exchange. (1)

Acceptance of it as a medium of exchange due to -

- It solves the problem of double coincidence of wants

- It is sometimes paid as advance with the promise of delivery of goods later. (1 + 1)

24. The Napoleonic Code was introduced with the purpose of bringing about significant administrative changes. It had the following features:

(a) It did away with all privileges based on birth.

(b) It established equality before law and secured the right to property.

(c) It simplified administrative division and abolished feudal system. (1 + 1 + 1)

25. Oilseeds usually have two main uses:

(a) They are used as a cooking medium as most of them are edible. For example, groundnut oil sunflower oil, coconut oil, etc.

(b) They are used as raw material. For example, oilseeds are important raw materials for the production of soap, cosmetics, ointments, etc.

   Gujarat is the largest producer of groundnut in India. (2 + 1)

26. • Government should ensure that labour laws are implemented properly

- Small producers should be supported to improve their productivity.

- Government can use trade and investment barriers, if needed. (1 + 1 + 1)

27. The three types of flows within international economy in exchanges were:

(a) Flow of Trade: Trade in tangible goods like wheat, cotton, etc. earlier fine cotton cloth was produced in India by weavers and exported to European countries.

(b) Flow of Labour: Migration of people in search of employment. A large number of Indian labourers migrated to Africa and other countries.

(c) Flow of Capital: Movement of capital over long distances for short-term and long-term investments. (1 + 1 + 1)

OR

The technological changes occurred slowly in Britain due to the following reasons:

(i) New technology was expensive and merchants and industrialists were cautious about using it.

(ii) The machines often broke down and repairs were costly.

(iii) They were not much effective as compared to cheap labour. (1 + 1 + 1)

28. Democracy is a process and development is the outcome. Democracy has a positive impact on economic and social development through mostly indirect channel. The channels include policy certainly; political stability the establishment and enforcement of rules that protect properly rights, the promotion of education and the ability promote private capital and the reduction of inequality. In democracies, time is taken on discussion and reaching at a decision so as to ensure maximum development.

OR

The problems faced by the political parties in India are as follows:

(a) Lack of Internal Democracy:- Although democracy functions with the help of political party but very often lack of internal democracy within the party can be seen. Generally the power within the party is concentrated in the hands of one or two leaders .

(b) Dynastic Succession: The biggest challenge between the political parties is the issue of dynastic succession. These parties do not have transparent functioning which is why the leaders always try to give unfair advantage to their family members.

(c) Money and Muscle Power: Another challenge which political parties face is the increased role of money and muscle power especially at the time of elections. Parties these days try to nominate that person as the candidate who is either rich or has sufficient muscle power behind him.

(d) Lack of Meaningful Choice: Political party generally discuss problems which the country is facing and their policy to resolve that problem. They always try to convince the general masses that their policies are better than the other parties. Differences arise only on priority of issue and how these policies are framed. All the political parties are same in one way or the other which is why people don't have any meaningful choice among them.

(Any three)$(1 + 1 + 1)$

SECTION C

29.
- 130 million hectares.
- Deforestation due to mining.
- Mineral processing like grinding of limestone.
- Overgrazing.
- Over irrigation. $(1 + 1 + 1 + 1 + 1)$

30.
- Political parties contest elections.
- They put forward policies and programmes and voters choose from them.
- They form and run government.
- They provide access to government machinery and welfare schemes.
- They play the role of opposition. $(1 + 1 + 1 + 1 + 1)$

31. Gandhi ji decided to launch a nation-wide Satyagraha:

(i)   This Act had been hurriedly passed through the Imperial Legislative Council.

(ii)   Indian members opposed the Act.

(iii) It gave the government enormous powers to repress political activities.

(iv) It allowed detention of political prisoners without trial for two years.

(Any two points to be explained.)

It opposed in the following ways:

(i)   Rallies were organised in various cities.

(ii)   Workers went on strike.

(iii) Shops were closed.

(iv) Communication, railway, telegraphs lines were disrupted.

(v)   Any other relevant point. (Any three) $(2 + 3 = 5)$

OR

Impact of the print revolution in Europe during the 15th and 16th century:

(i)   Printing reduced the cost of books.

(ii)   The time and labour required to produce each book came down, multiple copies could be produced with greater ease.

(iii) Books flooded the market, reaching out to an ever-growing readership.

(iv) Publishers started publishing popular ballads folk tales with beautiful pictures and illustrations.

(v)   Knowledge was transferred orally.

(vi) Print created the possibility of the wide circulation of ideas and introduced a new world of debate and discussion.

(vii) Even those who disagreed with established authorities could now print and circulate their ideas. e.g., Martin Luther was a German monk, priest, professor and church reformer. He challenged the Church to debate his ideas.

(viii) This led to division within the Church and the beginning of the Protestant Reformation.

(ix) Print and popular religious literature stimulated many distinctive individual interpretations of faith even among little-educated working people.

(x)   In the sixteenth century, Menocchio, a miller in Italy, reinterpreted the message of the Bible and formulated a view of God and Creation that enraged the Roman Catholic Church.

(Any five) $(1 \times 5 = 5)$

32. Sources

- Agriculture traders.
- Co-operative Societies.
- Money lenders.
- Relatives and friends.
- Commercial banks. (3)

The most popular is money lender because.

- No need of documentation.
- No collateral security is required. (2)

OR

- Exorbitant rate of interest
- Exploitative practices
- Amount is generally higher than the income
- High cost of borrowing

33. (a) Sri Lanka became independent in 1948. It immediately adopted measures to impose Sinhala supremacy. The Tamils felt alienated. No respect or recognition was given to their language, culture and religion.

(b) They began a struggle for equality in jobs, entry to the university, recognition of their language and culture.

(c) Slowly the conflict changed into a demand for regional autonomy.

(d) The Tamils were grouped together in the north and east of Sri Lanka.

(e) Their demands were ignored, the conflict became more severe and by the 1980s, their demands had changed.

(f) They wanted Tamil Eelam in the north and east. A civil war ensued, which killed thousands on both sides.

(g) The flourishing economy of Sri Lanka disappeared and the conflict gave blow to the social, cultural and economic life of Sri Lanka. (Any five) $(1 + 1 + 1 + 1 + 1)$

34. The secondary sector transforms raw materials into commodities. It is the second largest sector of our country.

Role in economic development:

(a) Secondary sector uses mechanical power and modern use of labour.

(b) It provides employment to a large number of people.

(c) It also helps in creating self-sufficiency in the country. It produces goods for local and international consumers. $(2 + 3)$

Section D

35. (a)   (A)   Chauri Chaura   (3 + 3)

       (B)   Amritsar

       (C)   Calcutta

35. (b)   (1)   Neyveli

       (2)   Singrauli

       (3)   Vijayanagara

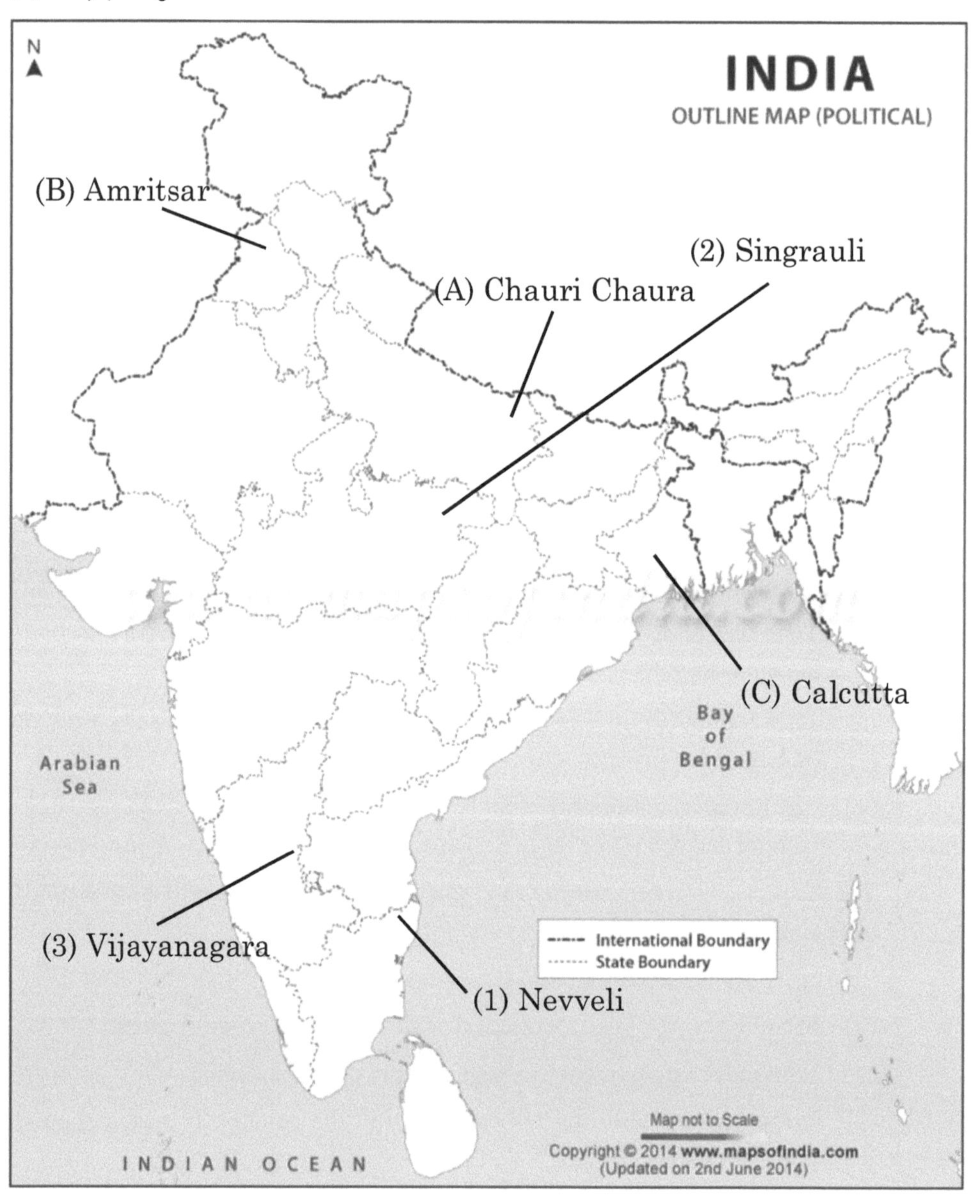

CBSE
Sample Question Paper 5

Social Science
Class X

Time : 3 hrs   **MM : 80**

SECTION A

1. Which one of the following types of government was functioning in France before the Revolution of 1789?   1

    (i) Democratic

    (ii) Republic

    (iii) Monarchy

    (iv) Anarchy

2. Which one of the following is the main cause of land degradation in Punjab? 1

    (i) Intensive cultivation

    (ii) Over irrigation

    (iii) Deforestation

    (iv) Overgrazing

3. In our country, NREGA 2005 aims to provide to all those who are able to, and are willing to work, a minimum of - 1

    (i)   100 days of employment in a year

    (ii) 200 days of employment in a year

    (iii) 120 days of employment in a year

    (iv) None of the above

4. Who wrote about the injustices of the caste system in 'Gulamgiri'? 1

    (i)   Raja Ram Mohan Roy

    (ii) Jyotiba Phule

    (iii) Bal gangadhar Tilak

    (iv) Bankim Chandra Chattopadhyay

5. Khan Abdul Ghaffar Khan led the Civil Disobedience Movement in Peshawar. 1

6. Coal is not a fossil fuel. 1

7. All intermediate goods and services produced during a year are counted in the national income. 1

8. In 1991, the Indian government decided to remove barriers on foreign trade and foreign investment. 1

9. One-third representation is given for women in India in local self-governments. 1

10. The French revolution transferred the sovereignty from the monarch to the _____________. 1

11. Communalism refers to a division based on_____________________________. 1

12. _____________has become the world's largest producer and consumer of steel. 1

13. NHAI is responsible for building _______________ highways. 1

14. Foreign affairs fall under ______________ list. 1

15. The newspaper by Bal Gangadhar Tilak was called as______________. 1

16. What does 'Silk Route refer to? 1

OR

Which Indian port lost its importance during colonial rule?

17. When wasNational Jute Policy formulated? 1

18. What are the two forms of modern currency? 1

19. In which country the principle of Majoritarianism led to a civil war? 1

20. Which industry, due to its seasonal nature, is ideally suited to the cooperative sector? 1

SECTION B

21. What were the effects of abolishing the 'Corn Laws (3)

OR

Why had the Surat and Hoogly ports declined by the end of 18th century? Explain any three reasons.

22. What is Agenda 21? List its two principles. (3)

23. Examine the holding together nature of Indian federation. (3)

24. Democracy is a better form of government than any other form of government – justify. (3)

25. Define balance of trade. Distinguish between favourable and unfavourable balance of trade. (3)

26. Give the benefits enjoyed by a local company in a Joint production with a MNC. (3)

27. Why did the Roman Catholic Church began to keep an Index of prohibited books from the mid 16th century? (3)

28. State the three features of intensive farming. (3)

Section C

29. Explain the features of the Boycott and Swadeshi movement.   (5)

OR

Write the difference between Non-co-operation and Civil Disobedience Movements?   (5)

30. Where is forest soil found? How does the texture vary according to the environment?   (5)

31. Suggest some reforms to strengthen parties so that they perform their functions well.   (5)

OR

Describe the role of citizens in a democracy.

32. How do banks play an important role in the economy of India? Explain.   (5)

33. "Caste has not still disappeared from contemporary India." Support the statement with suitable examples.   (5)

34. What is Sustainable Development? Explain any four measures to promote sustainable development.   (5)

Section D

35. (a) Two items A and B are shown in the given political outline map of India. Identify these items with the help of following information and write their correct names on the lines marked on the map.

(A) The place where Congress session was held in 1920   (1)

(B) The place where movement of indigo planters took place   (1)

On the same political map, locate and label the following:

(C) The place where Cotton mill workers Satyagraha took place.   (1)

35. (b) Two items (1) and (2) are shown in the given political outline map of India. Identify these items with the help of following information and write their correct names on the lines marked on the map.

(1) A sugar producing state   (1)

(2) A rubber producing state   (1)

On the same political map, locate and label the following:

(3) Talcher (1)

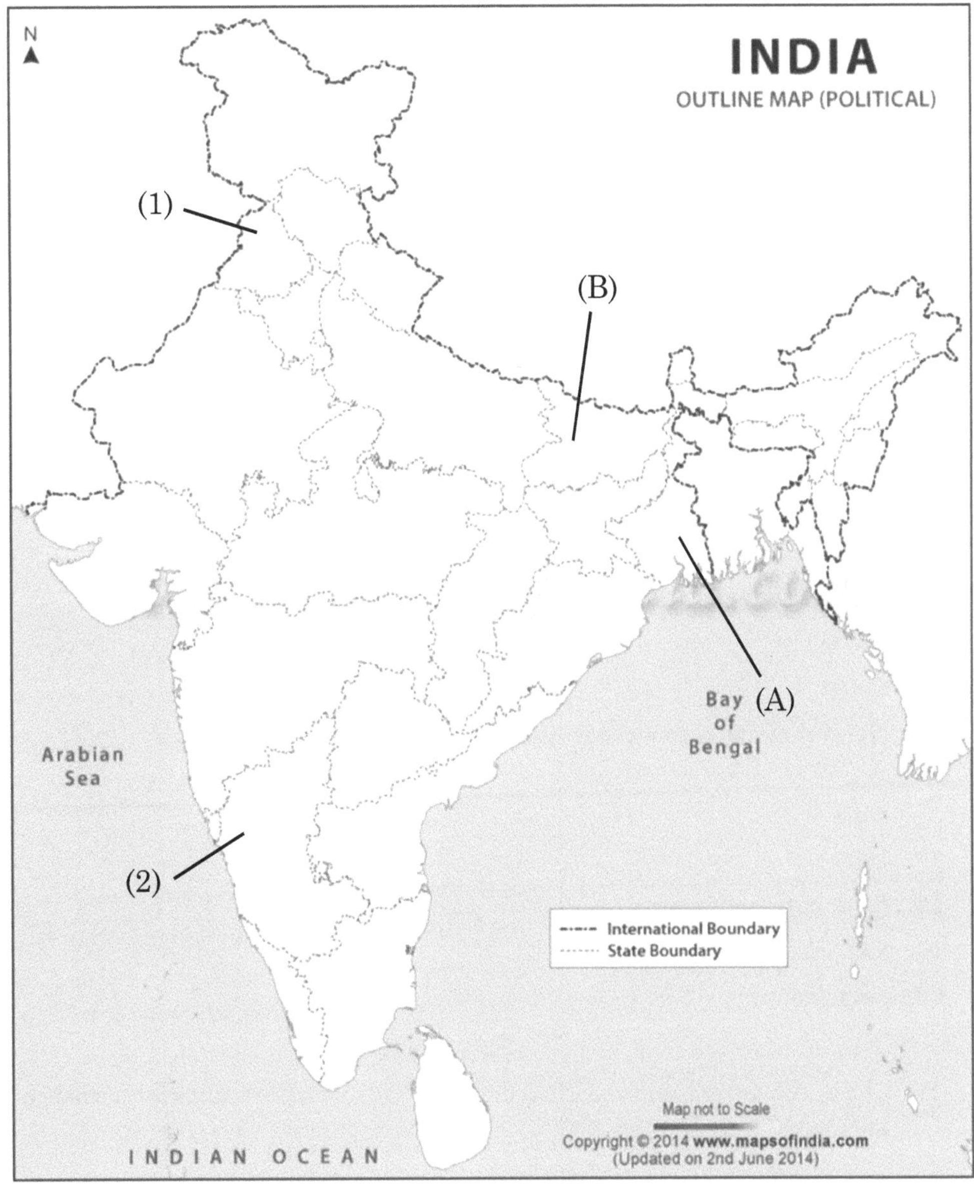

Solution

SECTION A

1. (iii) Monarchy (1)
2. (ii) Over irrigation (1)
3. (i) 100 days of employment in a year (1)
4. (ii) Jyotiba Phule (1)
5. True (1)
6. False (1)
7. False (1)
8. True (1)
9. True (1)
10. People (1)
11. Religion (1)
12. China (1)
13. Super Highways (1)
14. Union List (1)
15. Kesari (1)
16. Network of routes connecting Asia with Europe and Northern Africa (1)

OR

Surat

17. 2005 (1)
18. Paper notes and coins (1)
19. Sri Lanka (1)
20. Sugar industry (1)

SECTION B

21. The British government abolished the Corn Laws which brought a lot of changes in the British economy:

    (a) Food could be imported into Britain more cheaply than it could be produced within the country.

    (b) British agriculture failed to compete with imports.

    (c) Vast areas of land were left uncultivated.

    (d) Thousands of men and women became unemployed.

    (e) This led to migration of people to the cities or overseas.

    (f) Nations like Australia, Russia etc sent food grains to meet British demands. (½ × 6)

OR

(a) The port of Surat declined mainly because of the growing power of the European Companies in India.

(b) These European Companies gradually gained power and started to control sea-trade in India.

(c) They secured a variety of concessions which they obtained from the local courts and by gaining monopoly rights to trade. $(1 + 1 + 1)$

22. (i) Agenda 21 is the declaration signed by world leaders n 1992 at the United Nations Conference on Environment and Development (UNCED), which took place at Rio de Janeiro, Brazil.

(ii) The two principles of Agenda 21 are as follows :

    (a) To combat environmental damage, poverty and disease through global cooperation on common interests, mutual needs and shared responsibilities.

    (b) Every local government should draw its own local Agenda 21. $(1 + 2 = 3)$

23.
- States have not been given identical powers with union government.
- Few states like Jammu and Kashmir and North eastern states have been given special status.
- Some territories like Chandigarh and Delhi are administered by the uniongovernment.

$(1 + 1 + 1)$

24.
- It enhances the dignity of an individual.
- It involves every person in the decision making.
- It provides room to correct its own mistakes and resolve conflicts. $(1 + 1 + 1)$

25.
- The difference between export and import is known as balance of trade.
- If the value of export is more than the value of import it is favorable balance of trade.
- If the value of import is more than the value of export it is unfavorable balance of trade.

$(1 + 1 + 1)$

26.
- MNC can provide money for buying machines.
- MNC can provide latest technology.
- Local company will have access to international market. $(1 + 1 + 1)$

27. The Roman Catholic Church began keeping an index of Prohibited books from the mid-sixteenth century because its authority was being put in danger by the several individual and distinctive readings and questionings of faith prompted by the easily accessible popular religious literature. To supplement its inquisition and repression of heretical ideas, the Roman Catholic Church exercised strict control over publishers and booksellers, and also began to keep an Index of Prohibited Books from 1558. (3)

28. Features of intensive farming are:

(a) High yielding variety (HYV) seeds, modern chemical inputs and irrigation methods are used to increase the production.

(b) The per hectare yield is very high.

(c) More than one crop is cultivated during a year   (1+1+1)

SECTION C

29. • British institutions and services were denied by students, teachers and lawyers.

• Picketing of foreign liquor.

• Bonfire of foreign cloth.

• Refusal of traders to deal in foreign goods.

• Reduction in imports of cloth. $(1 + 1 + 1 + 1 + 1)$

OR

Non co-operation – 1920 – 1922

Reason – Jalianwala Bagh Tragedy

Methods – surrender of titles, boycott

Aim – Swaraj

Participation – All sectors

Civil Disobedience – 1930 – 1934

Reason – Arrival of Simon Commission

Methods – Breaking of colonial rules

Aim – Purna Swaraj

Participation – Dalits, Muslims and Industrial workers did not join.

30. • Found in hilly and mountainous areas.

• In the valley sides the soil is loamy and silty.

• It is coarse in upper slopes.

• In Himalayas soil is acidic with low humans content.

• It is fertile in the lower parts of the valley. $(1 + 1 + 1 + 1 + 1)$

31. • A law should be made to regulate the internal affairs of political parties.

• There should be state funding of elections.

• People, pressure groups and media can put pressure by petitions and agitations.

• Banning of political parties formed on the basis of religion and caste.

• It should be mandatory to all parties to allot one-third of the tickets to women.

$(1 + 1 + 1 + 1 + 1)$

OR

The roles of citizens in a democracy are as follows :

(i)   Citizens exercise their rights and freedoms and get benefited from the democratic setup.

(ii) They must be aware of their rights and duties.

(iii) They should be aware of the issues and problems the country is facing.

(iv) They must cooperate in maintaining law and order.

(v)   People must consider other's needs and interests also.

$(1 \times 5 = 5)$

32. Banks play an important role in developing the economy of India :

(i)   They keep the money of the people in their safe custody.

(ii) They give interest on the deposited money to the people.

(iii) They mediate between those who have surplus money and those who are in need of money.

(iv) They provide loan to a large number of people at the low interest rate.

(v)   They promote agricultural and industrial sector by providing loans.

(vi) They also provide funds to different organisations.   (Any five) $(1 \times 5 = 5)$

33. It is correct to say that "Caste has not still disappeared from contemporary India

(i)   Most people marry within their own caste or tribe.

(ii) Untouchability has not ended despite provisions in the constitution.

(iii) Effects of centuries of advantages and disadvantages continue to be felt today.

(iv) A large mass of low caste people still do not have access to education.

(v)   Caste is continued to be linked to economic status. $(1 + 1 + 1 + 1 + 1)$

34. Sustainable development is development that meets the needs of the present without compromising the ability of future generations to meet their own needs.

(i)   Increased use of renewable resources: Sustainable development is the management of renewable resources for the good of the entire human and natural community. For sustainable development, we must support the usage of renewable resources such as solar, wind, geothermal, and biomass energy sources.

(ii) Less use of fossil fuels: Fossil fuels take a lot of time to be formed. These fossil fuels contribute tremendously to environmental pollution.

(iii) Introduction of organic farming: Organic Farming contributes largely in creating a better quality of soil and combating erosion.

(iv) Adopting measures to reduce global warming: In our everyday life, we should contribute towards building a better environment. $(1 + 4)$

Section D

35. (a)   (A)   Calcutta   (3+3)
          (B)   Champaran
          (C)   Ahmedabad

35. (b)   (1)   Punjab   (3+3)
          (2)   Singrauli
          (3)   Talcher

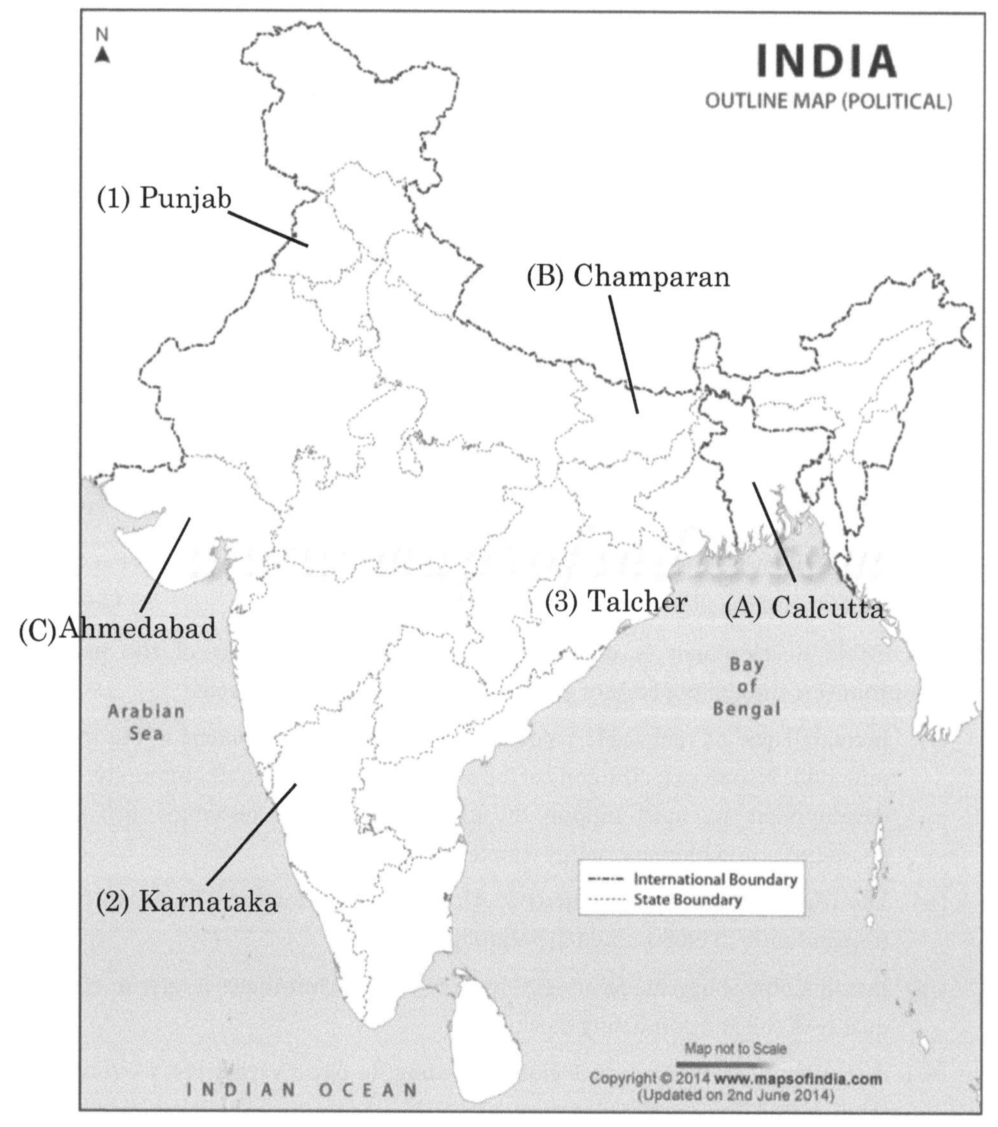

CBSE
Sample Question Paper 6

Social Science
Class X

Time : 3 hrs **MM : 80**

Section A

1. Napoleonic Code was introduced in _______________.　　　1

2. _______________ type of government has two or more levels.　　　1

3. Kakrapar nuclear power station is located in the state of_______________.　　　1

4. HDI stands for _______________.　　　1

5. Old alluvial soil is also called as _______________.　　　1

6. The capital of Belgium is ______________.   1

7. NREGA was passed in the year________________.   1

8. Workers from ____________ sector are generally underpaid.   1

9. Treaty of Vienna was signed in which year?   1

   (i) 1990

   (ii) 1817

   (iii)1820

   (iv) 1815

10. The first textile mill in India was established at: 1

   (i) Mumbai

   (ii) Karnataka

   (iii)Rajasthan

   (iv) Himachal Pradesh

11. Which of the following is prohibited by the Indian Constitution?   1

   (i) Discrimination only on the basis of gender

   (ii) Discrimination only on the basis of caste

   (iii)Discrimination on the basis of gender, religion and caste

   (iv) Discrimination on the basis of literacy level

12. Primary sector is considered as the highest in terms of providing employment
opportunities.   1

13. Iron ore is a non renewable resource.   1

14. Modern currency includes gold coins.   1

15. Trinamool Congress is a regional party of Kerala   1

16. What disease affected People's livelihood and local economy in Africa?   1

OR

What was the period before or beginning of industrialization known as?

17. Who was Martin Luther? 1

18. Which form of government is considered best? 1

19. What is the idea behind the development of Special Economic Zones (SEZs) in India? 1

20. What do you understand by economic growth? 1

SECTION B

21. Why did Industrial production in India increased during the First World War? 3

OR

Explain the impact of First World War over Britain's economy?

22. What are the three stages of resource planning in India? 3

OR

Describe the three cropping seasons in India. 3

23. What is multi party system? Why has India adopted a multi party system ? Explain. 3

24. How is "democratic government" is a legitimate, responsive and accountable government? Explain with example. 3

25. What is human development index? What are its basic components? Explain. 3

26. How does caste influence politics? 3

27. Explain the functions of Reserve Bank of India. 3

28. Explain any three advantages of globalization. 3

OR

How did the civil Disobedience Movement differ from Non-Cooperation Movement?

Section C

29. How far is it right to say that print culture was responsible for French Revolution. Explain. *5*

30. In which region are most of the jute mills of India concentrated and Why? What are the challenges faced by this industry? What steps have resulted in the increase of the internal demands of jute in the recent years? *5*

31. Suggest any five effective measures to reform political parties. *5*

32. "Self Help Groups" help borrowers to overcome the problem of lack of collateral. Explain the statement. *5*

OR

Describe any five provisions of 'National Rural Employment Guarantee Act 2005'.

33. Who hosted 'Vienna Congress' in 1815? Analyse the main changes brought by the 'Vienna Treaty. *5*

34. What type of soil is found in the river deltas of the eastern coast? Give four main features of this type of soil. *5*

Section D

35. (a) Two items A and B are shown in the given political outline map of India. Identify these items with the help of following information and write their correct names on the lines marked on the map.

    (A)   The place where Congress session was held in 1927 *1*

    (B)   The place where Cotton mill workers Satyagraha took place *1*

On the same political map, locate and label the following:

    (C)   Champaran *1*

(b) Two items (1) and (2) are shown in the given political outline map of India. Identify these items with the help of following information and write their correct names on the lines marked on the map.

    (1)   A Soil type *1*

    (2)   A nuclear plant *1*

On the same political map, locate and label the following:

(3)   Mayurbhanj   1

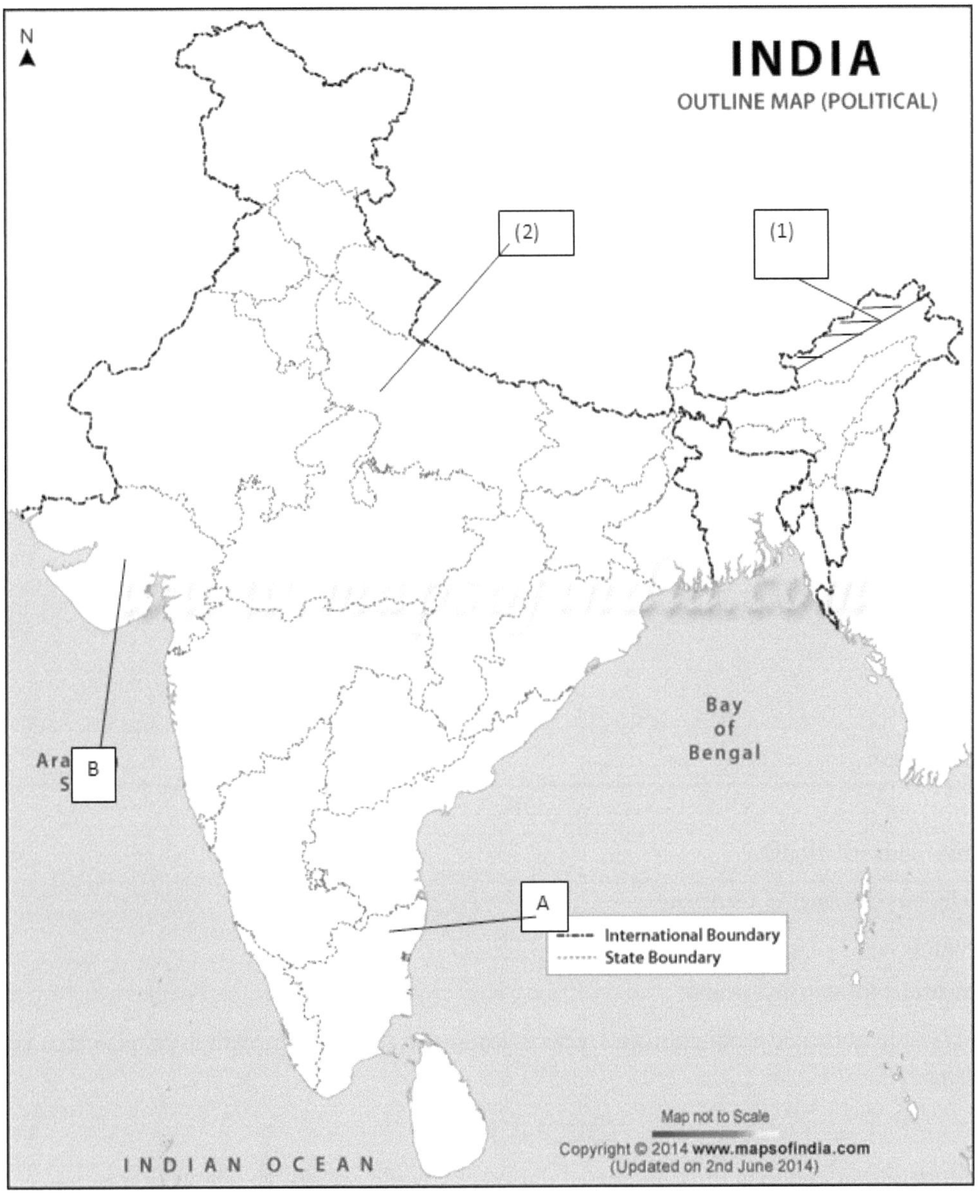

Solution

SECTION A

1. 1804 (1)
2. Federal (1)
3. Gujarat (1)
4. Human Development Index (1)
5. Bangar (1)
6. Brussels (1)
7. 2005 (1)
8. Unorganised sector (1)
9. (iv) 1815 (1)
10. (i)   Mumbai (1)
11. (iii) Discrimination on the basis of gender, religion and caste (1)
12. True (1)
13. True (1)
14. False (1)
15. False (1)
16. Rinderpest (1)

OR

Proto-industrialization

17. Religious reformer of Germany (1)
18. Democracy (1)
19. To attract foreign investment (1)
20. Increase in domestic production and services leading to all - round growth in people's standard of living. (1)

SECTION B

21. Industrial production in India ,increased during first world war due to following reasons-

    (i) With British mills busy with war production to meet the needs of the army, Manchester imports into India declined. Suddenly, Indian mills had a vast home market to supply .

    (ii) As the war prolonged, Indian factories were called upon to supply war needs: jute bags, cloth for army uniforms, tents and leather boots, horse and mule saddles and a lot of other items.

(iii) New factories were set up and old ones ran multiple shifts. Many new workers were employed and everyone was made to work longer hours. Over the war years industrial production boomed . (3)

OR

The First World War had a very bad impact on the British economy. Some of the effects are as follows:

(i) 15-25% part of their stockpiled wealth was spent on the war and after the war, they had to suffer massive debts, especially from US.

(ii) Britain had many buyers before the war. But after the war, it realized that its many buyers did not need to buy foreign buyers during the war.

(iii) The farmers also suffered because of the war as they had to produce more crops in the period of war but when the war was ended, they had excess stock of the crops. As a result of it, prices got declined and farmers had to face a great lose.

(iv) In the period of war, many industries failed to modernize. (3)

22. The stages of resource planning are:

(i) First we have to prepare inventory of resources which involves surveying, mapping and measurement of characteristics properties of resources.

(ii) Second we have to measure in terms of availability for development i.e. examining resources from the points of view of technology, economy and need.

(iii) At last we have to plan for exploitation of resources which involves action-oriented planning where the main emphasis is on use and reuse of the sources. (3)

OR

The cropping seasons of india can be explained as

Rabi season: Crops sown in winters and harvested in summers. Some of the important rabi crops are wheat, barley, peas, gram and mustard.

Kharif season: Crops grown with the onset of monsoons and harvested in September or October. Crops grown during this season are - rice, maize, jowar, bajra, tur, moong, urad, cotton, jute, groundnut and soyabean.

Zaid season: It falls in between the rabi and kharif seasons. Major crops grown are - watermelon, muskmelon, cucumbers, vegetables and fodder crop. (3)

23. A multi party system is a system where multiple political parties exist and have a chance of leading the government by contesting election .To ensure the sharing of the power among different section of society based on ideology ,tenets ,religions etc, India adopted the multi party system. (3)

24. Democracy is all about using the right to choose or vote. A democratic government is dependent on people's viewpoint. A leader is only able to win the democratic country, if he or she has given

the value to the people by people, right from the next day citizen started evaluating their deeds and the process became very transparent. So transparency is the main factor of a democratic government by which a leader needs to be very responsive to the needs and expectation of the citizens. (3)

25. Human Development Index is a tool developed by the United Nations to measure and rank countries based on   the level of social and economic development.

Three major indicators of the HDI are as follows.

(a) **Health:** Without proper health facilities, no matter how much a country earns, it will not be able to provide basic facilities to its people.

(b) **Education:** Over the past few decades, education has become an important factor in leading a quality life. So, if the country has high income but the literacy rate is low, it cannot be considered developed.

(c) **Per Capita Income:** It is the average income of each and every citizen and can be calculated by dividing the national income by population. Income is considered to be one of the most important indicators for development. (3)

26. Influence of caste on politics:

(a) While choosing candidates for election, political parties consider the caste composition of the voters to win support.

(b) When the government is formed, political parties take care that representative from different castes find place in the government.

(c) Political parties make appeal to the caste sentiments to win votes.

(d) Some political parties are known to favour some particular caste.

(e) Universal adult franchise and the principle of one-person one-vote have compelled the political leaders to bring caste sentiments into politics to muster support. (Any three)

(1+1+1)

27. 1. RBI issues currency notes on behalf of the central government.

2. It supervises the functioning of formal source of loan .

3. It monitors the banks in actually maintaining cash balance. (3)

28. Globalization is the process or trend of increasing interaction between people or companies on a world wide scale with the help of various method of communication

i. It helped many large companies in India to turn into MNCs which are spreading their operations worldwide. Globalization has also created new opportunities for various companies like IT.

ii. There is a greater choice before the consumers who now enjoy products with improved quality at lower prices.

iii. Globalization also broadened minds. It has led to the flow of ideas across national boundaries. (3)

OR

The Civil Disobedience Movement differed from the Non-Cooperation Movement in the following ways.

(a) Non-Cooperation Movement was launched between 1920 and 1922, while the Civil Disobedience Movement continued from 1930 to 1934.

(b) The Non-Cooperation Movement was launched because of the anger of Jallianwalla Bagh tragedy and the Civil Disobedience Movement was launched to protest the arrival of the Simon Commission.

(c) Non-Cooperation Movement began with the surrender of titles, boycott of British institutions and goods, whereas Civil Disobedience Movement began with defying and breaking the colonial laws, like Salt Law.

(d) Non-Cooperation Movement aimed for swaraj or self-government. Civil Disobedience Movement demanded complete independence or Purna Swaraj.

(e) The Non-Cooperation Movement got the support of almost all sections of the society whereas Civil Disobedience Movement had many limitations. The dalits, Muslims, industrial workers and businessmen did not participate fully.   (3)

SECTION C

29. The print culture paved the way of French revolution by following ways-

(1) print popularised the ideas of the Enlightenment thinkers. Collectively, their writings provided a critical commentary on tradition superstition and despotism. They argued for the rule of reason rather than custom, and demanded that everything be judged through the application of reason and rationality. They attacked the sacred authority of the Church and the despotic power of the state. The writings of Voltaire and Rousseau were read widely; and those who read these books saw the world through new eyes of questioning, critical and rational which created the notion to uproot present system .

(2) print created a new culture of dialogue and debate. All values, norms and institutions were re-evaluated and discussed by a public that had become aware of the power of reason, and recognised the need to question existing ideas and beliefs. That led to the new idea of revolution .

(3) by the 1780s there was an outpouring of literature that mocked the royalty and criticised their morality. In the process, it raised questions about the existing social order.   (5)

Entire situation changed due to print culture, people now awaken to get their rights by revolution.

30. Most of the jute mills of India are concentrated in the Hugli basin in West Bengal. It is a 98 km long and 3 km wide belt along the Hugli river.

Following are the main reasons for this.

(a) Proximity to the jute producing areas of Ganga-Brahmaputra basin. West Bengal is the leading producer of raw jute in the country and provides the mills with the required raw material.

(b) Abundant water for the processing of raw jute.

(c) Cheap water transport, supported by a good network of railways and roadways, facilitates the movement of raw materials to the mills.

(d) Cheap labour from West Bengal and the adjoining states of Bihar, Odisha and Uttar Pradesh.

(e) Banking and insurance facilities available in the city of Kolkata.

(f) Port facilities in Kolkata for the export of jute goods.

Following are the challenges faced by the jute industry in India.

(a) Stiff competition from synthetic substitutes in the international market.

(b) Competition from other jute goods producing countries like Bangladesh, Philippines, Thailand, Egypt and Brazil.

(c) Decrease in demand for packing materials, jute carpets and high cost of production.

(d) Old and inefficient machinery.

The government has taken several measures to boost the production of jute goods in order to face the competition from synthetic fibres and from other countries producing jute. In 2005, the National Jute Policy has been formulated with the objective of expanding quality production and increase in use of jute. The policy of the mandatory use of jute packaging has resulted in the increase of internal demand of jute in recent years.   (5)

31. Five effective measures to reform political parties are as follows:

(i) Any candidate that has any pending conviction should be barred from contesting election.

(ii) All political parties should file income tax and the financial accounts must be audited, with that their accounts must be made public.

(iii) Introduction of party hoping law preventing an individual from defecting to another without seeking fresh mandate from the electorates.

(iv) All parties must create slots for women and people with disabilities, there should be a transparent and democratic selection of successors of leader

(v) Parties must encourage inner party democracy, and thus should have regular elections (5)

32. Self-Help Groups are informal associations of people who choose to come together to find ways to improve their living conditions. They help to build Social Capital among the poor, especially women. The most important functions of a Self-Help Groups are to encourage and motivate its members to save, to persuade them to make a collective plan for generation of additional income, and to act as a conduit for formal banking services to reach them. Such groups work as a collective guarantee system for members who propose to borrow from organised sources. which helps borrowers to take financial help without collateral.   (5)

OR

Provisions NREGA 2005.

(i)   100 days assured employment every year to each rural household.

(ii)   One-third of the proposed jobs to be reserved for women.

(iii)   If an applicant is not employed within 15 days, he/she is entitled to a daily unemployment allowance.

(iv)   The governments have to establish Central Employment Guarantee Funds and State Employment Guarantee Funds for the implementation of the scheme.

(v)   The scheme is to be extended to 600 districts.   (1+1+1+1+1)

33. Congress of Vienna was hosted by Austrian Chancellor Duke Metternich in 1815.

The following changes were made:

(i)   The Bourbon dynasty, which had been deposed during the French Revolution, was restored to power and France lost the territories it had annexed.

(ii)   A series of states were set up on the boundaries of France to prevent the French expansion in future. Thus, the kingdom of the Netherlands, which included Belgium, was set up in the north and Genoa was added to Piedmont in the south.

(iii)   Prussia was given important new territories on its western frontiers, while Austria was given control of northern Italy.

(iv)   The German confederation of 39 states that had been set up by Napoleon was left untouched.

(1 + 4)

34. Alluvial soil is found in the eastern coastal plains particularly in the deltas of the Mahanadi, the Godavari, the Krishna and the Kaveri rivers.

Main features of alluvial soil:

(i)   It is formed by the deposition of alluvium brought down by the east flowing peninsular rivers.

(ii)   It is highly fertile.

(iii)   It consists of various proportions of sand, silt and clay.

(iv)   It is rich in potash, phosphoric acid and lime but deficient in organic matter.   (1 + 4)

Section D

35.   (3 + 3)

   (a)   (A)   Madras

         (B)   Ahmedabad

   (b)   (1)   Forest and Mountainous

         (2)   Narora

         (3)   Mayurbhanj

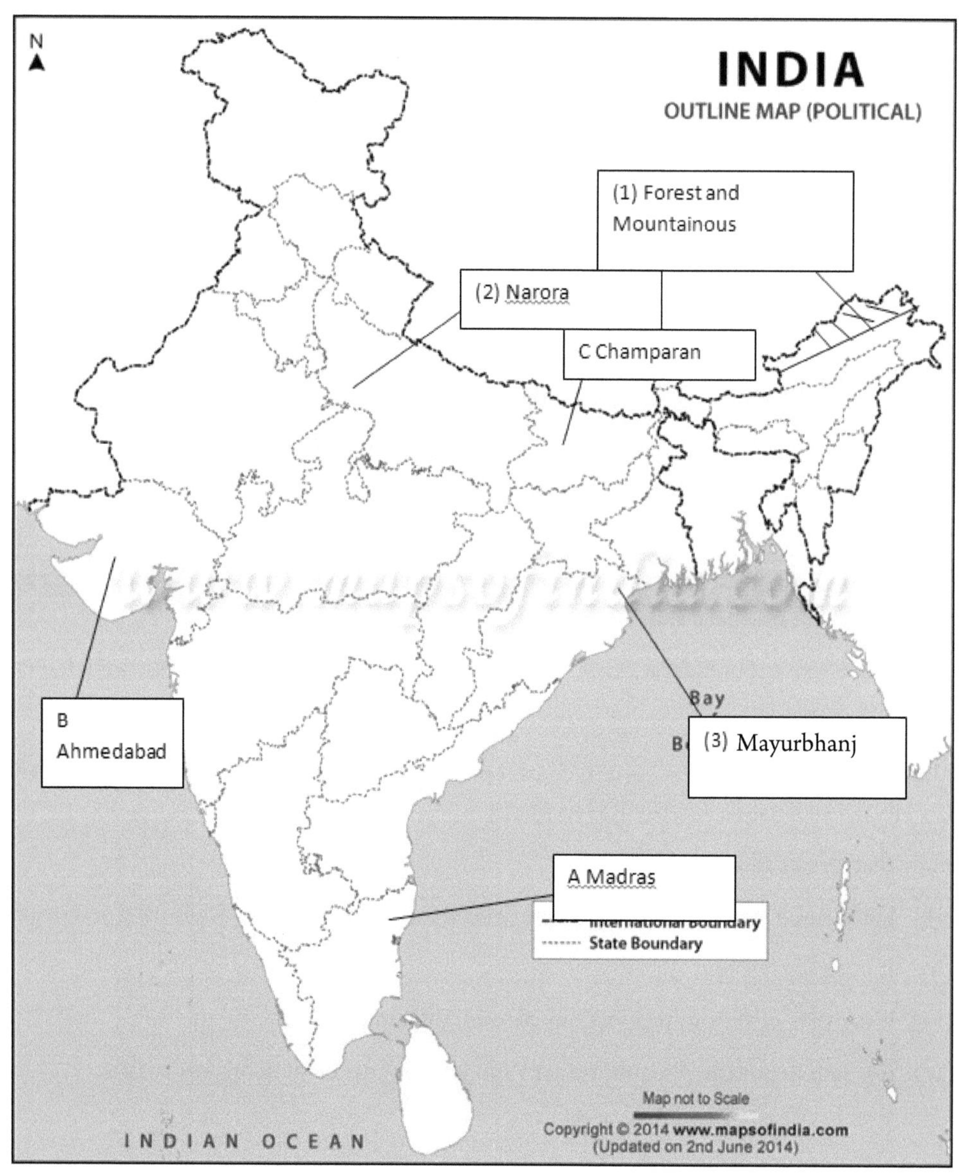

CBSE
Sample Question Paper 7

Social Science
Class X

Time : 3 hrs | **MM : 80**

SECTION A

1. Books in China were printed by rubbing paper against the inked surface of ______________.   1

2. ______________ has a 'Mayor' as its head.   1

3. ______________ transport is more popular in north-eastern India.   1

4. ______________ the most common indicator for measuring economic development of a country.   1

5. Iron and steel industry is a ______________ based industry.   1

6. India is a _________ income country.   1

7. The Prime Minister of India is chosen by __________.   1

8. Gram Panchayat is a part of _________ government.   1

9. Paper reached Europe from China in: 1

   (i) 12th century   (ii) 18th century

   (iii)11th century   (iv) 15th century

10. The oldest oil producing State of India is: 1

   (i) Mumbai   (ii) Assam

   (iii)Rajasthan   (iv) Kerala

11. Which of the following is a characteristic of power sharing?   1

   (i) Power is controlled by a single person

   (ii) It gives people the right to be consulted

   (iii)Parliament is above all

   (iv)All of the above

12. Primary sector is considered as the highest in terms of providing employment
opportunities.   1

13. Rice is one of the major crops grown in India.   1

14. Modern currency includes gold coins.   1

15. According to caste hierarchy all castes are equal.   1

16. Which two institutions are well known as Bretton Woods Institutions?   1

OR

Who invented the Spinning Jenny?

17. By whom was the Swaraj Party formed?   1

18. Who said 'Religion can never be separated from politics?   1

19. Give any two examples of industries from the tertiary sector.   1

20. What is the other name for underemployment?   1

SECTION B

21. Describe the impact of 'Rinderpest' on people's livelihoods and local economy in
Africa in the 1890s.   3

OR

Describe any three major problems faced by Indian cotton weavers in nineteenth
century.

22. "Dense and efficient network of transport is a pre-requisite for local and national development." Analyse the statement.   3

23. Describe any three provisions of amendment made in 'Indian Constitution' in 1992 for making 'Three-Tier' government more effective and powerful.   3

24. "Secularism is not an ideology of some political parties or persons, but it is one of the foundations of our country." Examine the statement.   3

25. What outcomes can one reasonably expect of democracies?   3

26. Average income is important but has its limitation while using it, Explain.   3

27. Give an account on MNERGA .   3

28. In spite of globalization creating good quality product and expanding market, how is it affecting stability in jobs for the workers?   3

OR

'Agriculture is the mainstay of the Indian economy.' Explain the statement by giving three points.

SECTION C

29. "Explain the attitude of the Indian merchants and the industrialists towards the 'Civil Disobedience Movement'.   5

30. Why is the economic strength of a country measured by the development of manufacturing industries ? Explain with example.   5

31. How has foreign trade been integrating markets of different countries ? Explain with examples.   5

OR

Explain the differences between formal and informal sources of credit.

32. Describe any five major functions of political parties performed in a democracy.   5

33. Describe the impact of Great Depression on Indian economy.   5

OR

What were the principal features of industrialisation process of England in the 19th century?

34. What are the climatic conditions required for the growth of rice?   5

SECTION D

35. (a) Two items A and B are shown in the given political outline map of India. Identify these items with the help of following information and write their correct names on the lines marked on the map.

     (A)   The place where Congress session was held in December 1920.   1

     (B)   The place where Mahatma Gandhi broke the salt law   1

On the same political map, locate and label the following:

    (C).   The place where the Non-cooperation movement was called off.   1

(b) Two items (1) and (2) are shown in the given political outline map of India. Identify these items with the help of following information and write their correct names on the lines marked on the map.

    (1)   Iron and steel industry plant   1

    (2)   A software technology park   1

On the same political map, locate and label the following:

    (3)   Tuticorin   1

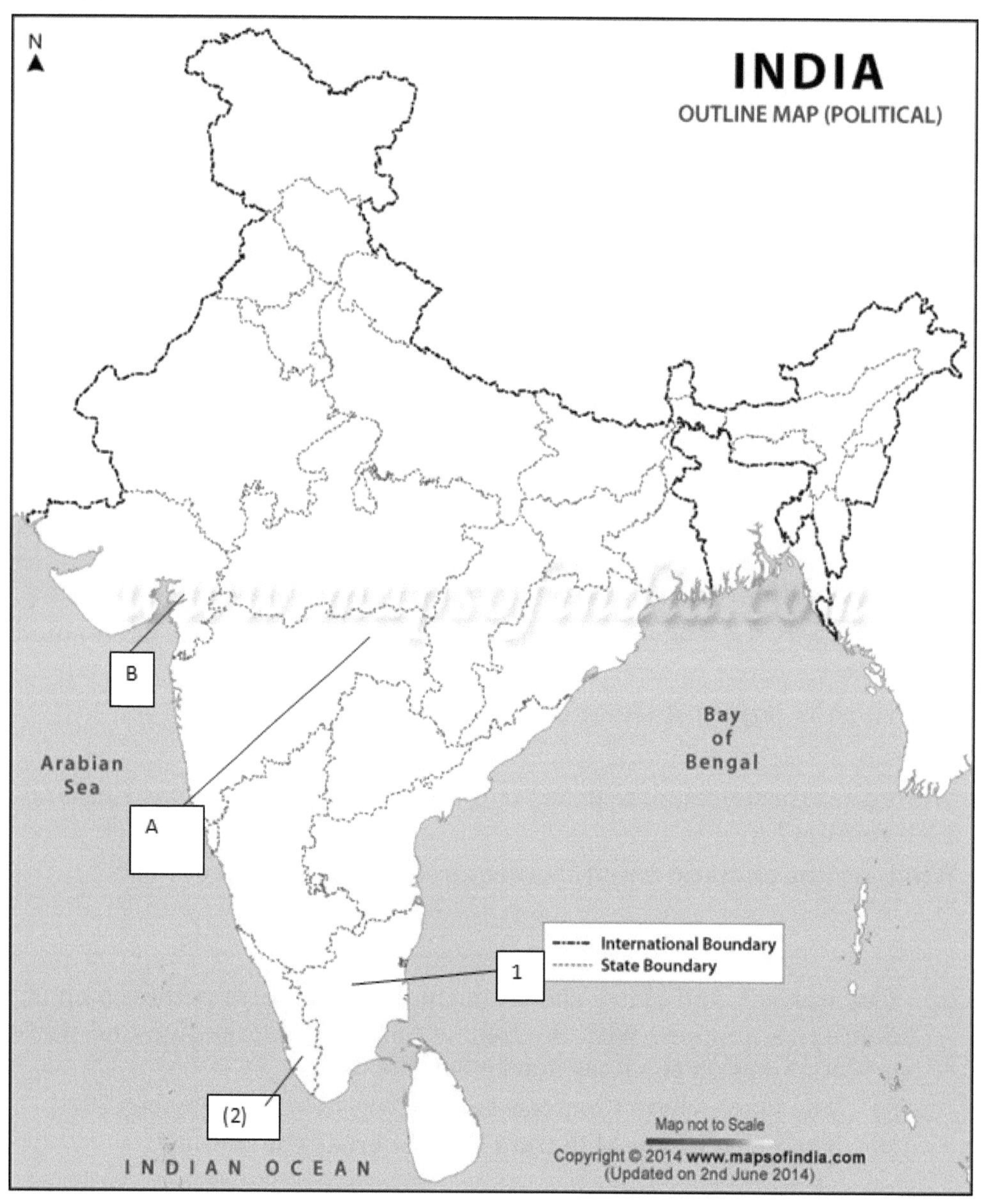

Solution

SECTION A

1. Woodblocks (1)
2. Municipal Corporation (1)
3. Air (1)
4. Per Capita income (1)
5. Mineral (1)
6. Low (1)
7. Elections (1)
8. Local (1)
9. (iii) 11th century (1)
10. (ii) Assam (1)
11. (ii) It gives people the right to be consulted (1)
12. True (1)
13. True (1)
14. True (1)
15. False (1)
16. IMF and World Bank (1)

OR

James Hargreaves

17. Motilal Nehru and C.R. Das (1)
18. Mahatma Gandhi (1)
19. Banking, transport (1)
20. Disguised unemployment (1)

SECTION B

21. Impact of Rinderpest on Africa-
    (i) 90% of cattle were killed by Rinderpest.
    (ii) Livelihood was destroyed due to loss of cattle.
    (iii) People were forced into labour market.
    (iv) European colonizers were able to conquer and subdue Africa when they got to control over cattle resources (3)

OR

Major problems faced by the Indian cotton weavers-
  (i) Their export market collapsed.
  (ii) The local market shrunk and **glutted with Manchester** products .
  (iii) There was increase in price of raw cotton.
  (iv) There was shortage of cotton.

    (v) It was difficult for weavers to compete with the imported machine made cheaper cotton products.

    (vi) Factories in India also began cheaper machine made goods to which our weavers could not compete　　　　　　　　　　　　　　　　　　　　　　　　　　　　　　(3)

22. Dense and efficient network of transport and communication is a pre-requisite for national and international trade because:

    (i) **Raw materials** can easily **reach** their **respective centers** of production by means of good transportation.

    (ii) **Good transport infrastructure** is very **important** to enable finished products to reach their respective markets.

    (iii) Communication **eases** the **integration of markets** and investments.

    (iv) **Communication** facilities are of utmost importance in tertiary activities like **providing knowledge** about **events happening** in distant places.　　　　　　　　(3)

23. Amendment in Indian Constitution in 1992-

    (i) It is **constitutionally mandatory to hold regular elections** to local government bodies.

    (ii) **Seats reserved** for the Scheduled Caste, Scheduled Tribes and Other Backward Classes.

    (iii) **At least one third of all positions are reserved** for **women.**

    (iv) **Creation of State Election Commission.**

    (v) The state governments are directed to **share some powers** and **revenue** with local government bodies.　　　　　　　　　　　　　　　　　　　　　　　　(3)

24. Secularism is the foundation of our country

    (i) There is **no official religion** of India.

    (ii) Our constitution **does not give a special status** to any religion.

    (iii) The constitution **prohibits discrimination** on ground of religion.

    (iv) The constitution provides all individuals and communities **freedom to profess, practice** and **propagate any religion** or not to follow any religion.

    (v) The constitution **allows the state to intervene in the matters of religion** in order to ensure equality.　　　　　　　　　　　　　　　　　　　　　　　　　(3)

25. The outcomes one can reasonably expect of the democracy are :

    (i) In the political sphere-Right to vote, Right to contest.

    (ii) In the economic sphere-Minimised economic inequalities.

    (iii) In the social sphere-Equal protection to women, SCs, STs and OBCs.　　$(1 \times 3 = 3)$

26. The **average income earned per person** in a given area in a year. This is used for **measuring development** of any country.

    Per Capita Income has **limitations** which include:

    1. **Covering only the economic aspect** and **ignoring factors like education, health, environment** etc.

    2. There is **no transparency regarding distribution of income.**　　　　　(3)

27. **National Rural Employment Guarantee Act 2005** or NREGA is a **social security measure** implemented by the **government of India** in **200 districts of the country, in starting** from 1ˢᵗApril 2008 it is implemented in all districts of India. It **ensures 100 days** of **employment in a year by the government** to all those who can work and **increases livelihood securities in local areas.** There is also a **provision of unemployment allowance** given to people. The **gram panchayat is responsible for official verification** of people under this act, 33% seats are reserved for women. (3)

28. (a) employment of flexible workers

(b) Increased competition, objective to lower costs, the axe falls on the labour cost temporary jobs given

(c) Longer working hours for labour to get suitable salaries (3)

OR

Agriculture is the mainstay of the Indian economy because :

(a) Two thirds of the population is dependent on agriculture. It generates large scale employment.

(b) It provides food for teeming millions.

(c) It provides raw materials to many agro-based industries like cotton, rubber, sugar.

(d) Export of agricultural products like tea and spices earns valuable foreign exchange.

(e) It contributes 26% of gross domestic product (GDP). (any three) (3)

SECTION C

29. The attitude of the Indian merchants and the industrialists towards the 'Civil Disobedience Movement' can be described as follows:

(i) Indian industrialists believed that t he colonial policies were restricting their business as they made huge profits during the **First World War.**

(ii) They refused to buy or sell any imported goods.

(iii) They were against all the trade barriers and wanted to expand their business at their own.

(iv) The organization **FICCI (Federation of the Indian Chamber of Commerce Industry)** was organized in **1927,** to look after their business interests.

(v) They wanted protection against imports of foreign goods and therefore, they were an active participant in the **'Civil Disobedience Movement'.** (5)

30. Democracy stands much superior to any other form of government in promoting the dignity and freedom of the individual.

(i) The passion for respect and freedom are the bases of democracy. Democracy accepts dignity of women as a necessary ingredient of society. We have historically had male dominated societies. There is sensitivity to women's issues because of long struggles by them. Democracy recognises **the principle of equal treatment to women** unlike non-democratic governments.

   (ii) Democracy in India has strengthened the claims of the disadvantaged and discriminated castes for equal status and opportunity, which is not possible in any non-democratic country.

   (iii) The same is true of caste inequalities. Democracy in India has strengthened the claims of the **disadvantaged and discriminated castes for equal status** and opportunity.

   (iv) Most societies were historically male dominating. The status of women was not satisfactory. After long struggles by women, democracy throughout the world has recognised equal treatment and respect to women at least in principles.

   (v) Also, democracy has to meet the expectations of citizens and people have the right to complain about the functioning of democracy. (5)

31. **Foreign trade** is all about **expanding the business beyond the domestic market.** Many foreign trader expand their business in other countries too, e.g. Initially the **toys are quite expen sive in India** which was **not affordable** for every household. **China took this as an advantage** and **brings their toys in cheap prices** and with different varieties, people like their product china get a good response from Indian market where as Indian toy seller get opposite response.

China get a good response from Indian market whereas **Indian toy seller get opposite response.** So with the opening trade **goods travel from one market to another.** Choice of goods in the Market rise and producer of two different countries get competent. Foreign trade thus result in Connecting the markets. (5)

OR

S.No.	Formal Sector Credit	Informal Sector Credit
(i)	Includes banks and cooperatives.	Includes moneylenders, traders, employers, friends and relatives.
(ii)	Banks require collateral and proper documentation for getting a loan.	No collateral is required.
(iii)	A reasonable rate of interest is charged.	Repeated borrowing, can lead to debt trap.
(iv)	Apart from profit making, they also have an objective of social welfare.	Their only motive is to extract profit as much as possible.
(v)	Terms of credit are fair and reasonable.	They impose very tough and sometimes even unreasonable terms of credit on borrowers.

(1+1+1+1+1)

32. 1. **It makes the working of parliamentary government** - The political parties participate in election, forms the government with majority votes and runs the state and the other parties in the legislature **constitute the opposition** and try to find fault with the government, thus making it more responsible.

2. **Political Parties formulate public policies.** Each political party fights the election to achieve its objectives incorporated in their political manifesto. These policies are made keeping in mind the interest of general public. The most important objective behind most policies remains the betterment of general condition. Other than this, they make policies on national security, internal law and order, etc. Besides, each party has its own ideology. It is assured that the majority party gets the mandate of the electorate to implement its own political programme.

3. **Political parties educate public opinion.** Parties in any system of government educate, formulate and organize public opinion. They also help in the growth of the **level of political consciousness** of common citizens, who otherwise have no time to peruse and study issues of the state. The political parties in their effort to come closer to the people organize public rallies, meetings, press conferences on important issues and make their views clear.

4. **Political parties provide political stability.** The political parties in more than one way unite, simplify and stabilized the political process of the country. The destabilizing forces of localism, regionalism, section, interests and geographical situations are tackled by political parties by making these parts of their party ideology thus **pacifying the disintegrating forces and inducing cohesion.** Besides the political parties in a representative democracy play a great role in maintaining the stability by performing their roles in the legislature. The majority party forms the government and the other small parties in the opposition.

5. **Political parties act as a government policy checker**: The party in power has to conduct itself very responsibly. The opposition party keeps a close eye on the working of the ruling party. Because any **unwise move on their part** would throw it off the power and help the opposition (parties) to take over the reins of administration. Opposition not merely criticizes the government; it also provides an alternative program and alternative government in the eventuality of any crisis in the government. As such it contributes to the **stability of the government.** Hence, healthy opposition is very important for the success of democracy.   (any three) $(1+1+1+1+1)$

33. The impact of Great Depression on Indian economy:

(i)   India's exports and imports nearly halved between 1928 and 1934.

(ii) As agricultural prices fell sharply internationally as a result of this prices plunged in India.

(iii) Despite of this, the colonial government refused to reduce revenue demands.

(iv) Peasants' indebtedness increased. They used up their savings, mortgaged lands and sold their jewellery and precious metals.

(v) India became exporter of metal.

(vi) Town dwellers found themselves better off.

(vii) Industrial investment grew.   (Any five)

                                                                      $(1 \times 5 = 5)$

OR

(i) Cotton industry grew rapidly followed by iron and steel industry.

(ii) Introduction of railways added to industrial growth.

(iii) New factories could not displace traditional industries.

(iv) Industries tried to improve their speed and quality of production.

(v) Implementation of technology happened at a slow rate

                                                                      $(1+1+1+1+1)$

34. Climatic conditions required for the growth of rice:

(i) It is a Kharif crop which requires high temperature (above 25°C).

(ii) It requires high humidity with annual rainfall above 100 cm.

(iii) In the areas of less rainfall, it grows with the help of irrigation.

(iv) It is grown in the plains of north and north-eastern India, coastal areas and deltaic regions.

(v) Development of dense network of canal irrigation and tubewells have made it possible to grow rice in areas of less rainfall such as Punjab and Haryana. $(1+1+1+1+1)$

Section D

35.   (3 + 3)

     (a)   (A)   Nagpur

            (B)   Dandi

            (C)   Chauri Chaura

     (b)   (1)   Salem

            (2)   Thiruvananthapuram

            (3)   Tuticorin

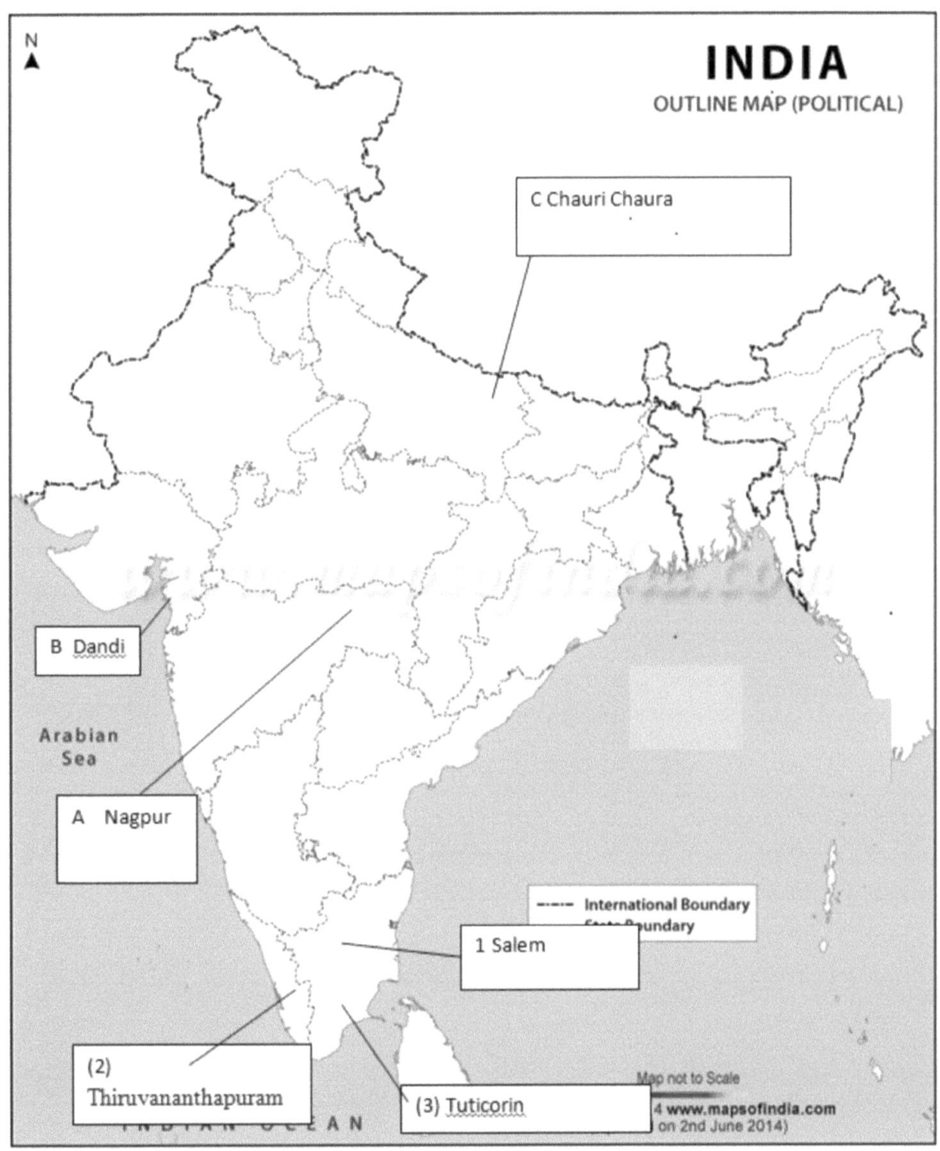

CBSE
Sample Question Paper 8

Social Science
Class X

Time : 3 hrs | MM : 80

General Instructions

i. The question paper has **35** questions in all.

ii. Marks are indicated against each question.

iii. Questions from serial number **1** to **20** are objective type questions. Each question carries **one mark**. Answer them as instructed.

iv. Questions from serial number **21** to **28** are **3 marks** questions. Answer of these questions should not exceed **80 words** each.

v. Questions from serial number **29** to **34** are **5 marks** questions. Answer of these questions should not exceed **120 words** each.

vi. Question number **35** is a map question of **6 marks** with two parts - **35 a.** from History (3 marks) and **35 b.** from Geography (3 marks).

SECTION A

1. The Rowlatt Act was passed in ______________. 1

2. A democratic government provides ______________ for arriving at a decision. 1

3. The management of resources by humans is known as ______________. 1

4. A deposit with a bank that can be withdrawn whenever the depositor likes to do so, is termed as ______________. 1

5. ______________ is a short crop season in between the Rabi and the Kharif season. 1

6. India is a ___________ state.   1

7. ______________ have higher rate of economic growth.   1

8. Bank is a ___________ source of credit.   1

9. What issue gave Mahatma Gandhi an opportunity to bring the Hindus and Muslims on a common platform?   1

   (i) Simon Commission

   (ii) Khilafat issue

   (iii)Sati

   (iv)Round table conference

10. The science and art of growing plants is known as: 1

   (i) Sericulture

   (ii) Slash and Burn

   (iii)Horticulture

   (iv)Orchid Farming

11. What type of party system exists in India?   1

   (i) Bi-party

   (ii) Single party

   (iii)Multi party

   (iv)Dictatorship

12. Removing barriers or restrictions set by the government is known as privatization.   1

13. Shaft mining is a form of underground mining.   1

14. Tata Motors is a foreign MNC.   1

15. The Election Commission is responsible for conducting free and fair elections in the country   1

16. By whom was 'Sambad Kaumudi' published in 1821?   1

17. From where did Marco Polo bring back the knowledge of woodblock printing to Italy?   1

18. What is an important function of political party?   1

19. What is GDP?   1

20. Who publishes the economic survey?   1

SECTION B

21. Explain the response of business class in India to the Civil Disobedience Movement.   3

OR

Describe the Peasant Rebellion in Awadh during the Non-Cooperation Movement.

22. Write the three properties of alluvial soil .   3

OR

Name the important beverage crop introduced by the british in india. Explain the geographical conditions needed for its cultivation.

23. How is MNC able to cope with large demands all over the world and control prices?   3

OR

How do Multi-National Corporations (MNCs) interlink production across countries? Give examples.

24. Give a brief about the three components of a political party.   3

25. "Money cannot buy all the goods and services that a person may need to live well". Explain the statement with suitable examples.   3

26. What is money? Why is modern money currency accepted as a medium of exchange?   3

27. Explain any three forms of communalism in the Indian politics.   3

28. What are the merits of Democracy?   3

SECTION C

29. Why was Congress reluctant to allow women to hold any position of authority within the organization? How did women participate in Civil Disobedience Movement? Explain.   5

30. "Fair globalisation is possible if the government plays a major role in making it possible." Support the statement.   5

31. "Democracy is seen to be good in principle but felt to be not so good in practice". Justify the statement.   5

32. Which is the most abundantly available fossil fuel in India? Assess the importance of its different forms.   5

33. What was Rinderpest? How did it impact the Africans?   5

OR

What was 'proto-industrialisation'? Explain the importance of proto-industrialisation

34. Why is it necessary to conserve mineral resources? Explain any four ways to conserve mineral resources.   5

SECTION D

35. (a) Two items A and B are shown in the given political outline map of India. Identify these items with the help of information given below:

    (A)   The place which is known for Cotton Mill Workers Satyagraha.   1

    (B)   The place where Congress Session was held in September 1920.   1

On the same map, locate and label the following:

    (C)   Champaran : The place known for Indigo Planters Movement.   1

(b) Two items (1) and (2) are shown in the given political outline map of India. Identify these items with the help of following information and write their correct names on the lines marked on the map.

    (1)   A rubber producing state   1

    (2)   A state which is the major producer of sugarcane   1

On the same political map, locate and label the following:

    (3)   Durg   1

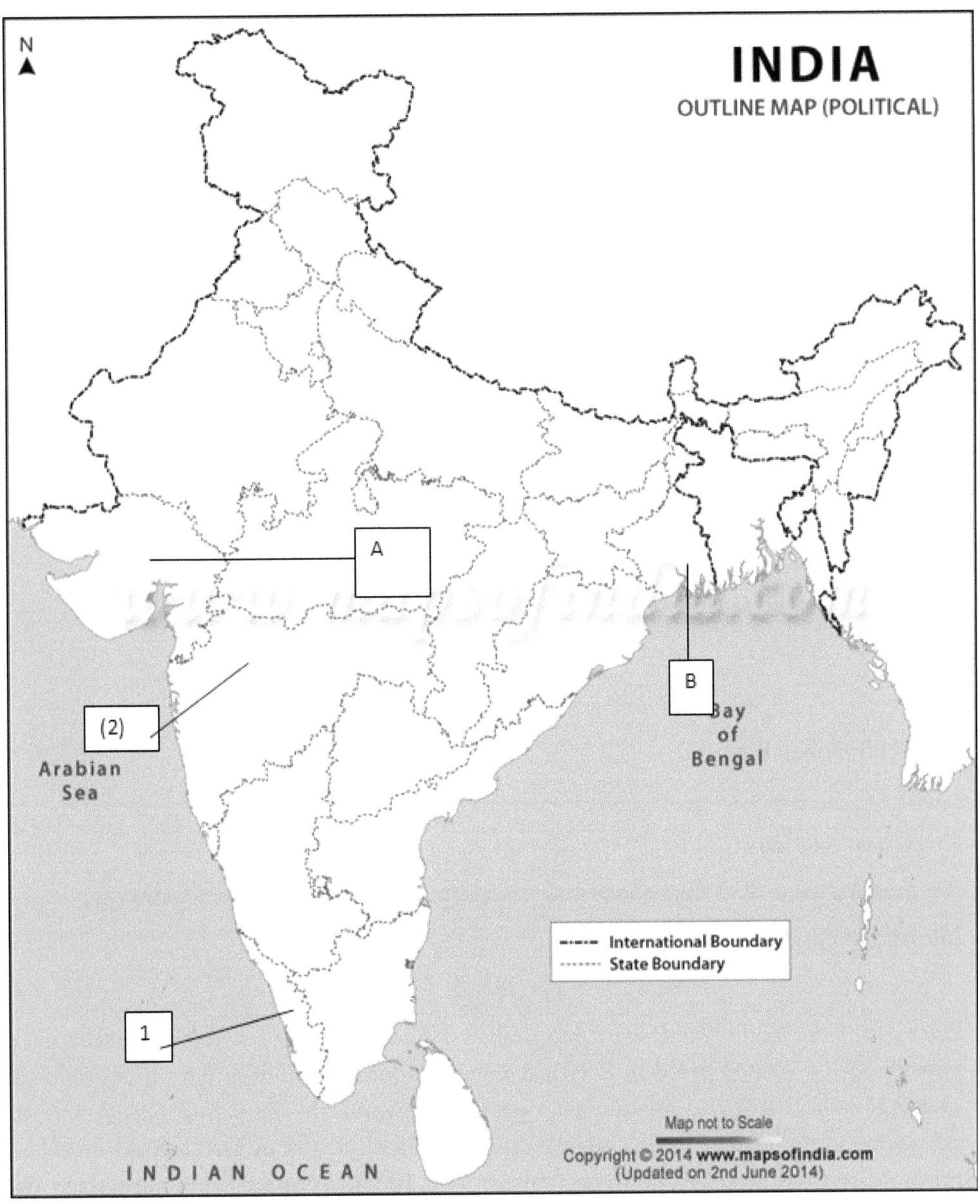

Solution

Section A

1. 1919 (1)
2. rules and procedures (1)
3. Conservation (1)
4. Demand deposit (1)
5. Zaid (1)
6. Secular (1)
7. Dictatorships (1)
8. Formal (1)
9. (ii) Khilafat issue (1)
10. (iii) Horticulture (1)
11. (iii) Multi party (1)
12. False (1)
13. True (1)
14. False (1)
15. True (1)
16. Raja Ram Mohan Roy (1)
17. China (1)
18. To contest elections (1)
19. It is the total value of all final goods and services produced during a particular year (1)
20. Ministry of Finance (1)

Section B

21. During the First World War, Indian merchants and industrialists had made huge profits and became powerful. They wanted protection against import of foreign goods and a rupee-sterling foreign exchange ratio that would discourage imports. To organize business interests, they formed the various organization like FICCI. Led by industrialists like Purshottamdas Thakurdas and G.D. Birla, the industrialists attacked colonial control over Indian economy and supported the Civil Disobedience Movement when it was first launched. They gave financial assistance and refused to buy or sell imported goods. Most businessmen came to see Swaraj as a time when colonial restrictions on business would no longer exist and trade and industry would flourish without constraints. But, after the failure of the Round Table Conference, business groups were no longer uniformly enthusiastic. (3)

OR

The Peasant Rebellion in Awadh was led by Baba Ramchandra, a 'Sanyasi', who was earlier a labourer in Fiji. Here, the movement was against 'talukdars' and landlords who demanded high rents from peasants. The peasants were forced to do 'begar' and work at farms of landlords with no wages. The Peasant Movement thus demanded reduction of revenue, abolition of 'begar' and the boycott of oppressive landlords. In 1920, Shri Jawaharlal Nehru toured Awadh villages to understand peasant grievances. This led to the formation of the Oudh Kisan Sabha headed by Shri Nehru and Baba Ramchandra. So, when the Non-Cooperation Movement began, the effort of the Congress was to integrate the Awadh peasants into the wider struggle   (3)

22. 1.   Alluvial soil is considered the most fertile soil.

    2.   Alluvial soil contains sand, silt and clay.

    3.   According to **age**, the alluvial soil is classified as Bangar (old alluvial) and Khadar.   (3)

OR

Tea is introduced by the British in India.   (3)

The geographical condition for cultivation-

The lowest temperature for the **growth of tea** is 16°C.

Rainfall: 150-250 cm of rainfall is **required** for **tea cultivation.**

Soil: **Tea** require fertile mountain soil mixed with lime and iron. The soil should be rich in humus

23. 1.   Large MNC in developed countries place order for the production with small producers.

    2.   The MNC's sell these products under their own name.

    3.   Due to the good quality of products prepared by small producers they control the market

With the huge demand and by controlling the huge demands MNC are able to control prices also.   (3)

OR

(i)   **MNCs buys local small companies** to sell their products in large area of the country. For example- Cargill foods bought Parakh , a smaller Indian company having a large marketing network in various part of India and become the largest producer.

(ii)   **Small industries produce raw material for these Multi-National Corporations** which helps them to grow as well.

(iii)   Sometimes, **money for advance investments** for setting up new machines **are provided by MNCs** to increase the production.   (3)

24. Three Components of a Political Party:

(i)   The Leaders: Every political party has some prominent leaders who prepare policies and programmes of the party and choose candidates for contesting elections.

 (ii) The Active Members: They are involved in different committees of the party and participate directly in their activity.

 (iii) The Followers: They believe in the party's ideology and support the party by casting their votes in favour of the party at the time of elections. (3)

25. Money cannot buy all the goods and services that a person may need to live well. Income by itself is not a completely adequate indicator of material goods and services that citizens are able to use. For example, normally, money cannot buy a pollution-free environment or ensure that a person gets unadulterated medicines, unless a person can afford to shift to a community that already has all these things. Money may also not be able to protect individual from infectious diseases, unless the whole of our community takes preventive steps. (3)

26. Something that acts as a **medium of exchange in transactions of goods and services** can be taken as **Money.** It also serves as a standard unit to determine their value.

 The government of the country has authorized the currency therefore **modern money currency is accepted as a medium of exchange** for easier transactions and promotion of trade.

 Indian rupee is widely accepted as a medium of exchange in India. The rupee currency notes issued on behalf of Indian government by the Reserve Bank of India, cannot be refused by anybody they have to accept rupees in exchange of goods and services in India (3)

27. Various forms of communalism in politics :

 (a) The most common expression of communalism is in every day beliefs.

 (b) A communal mind often leads to a pursuit for political dominance of one's own religious community.

 (c) Political mobilization on religious lines is another common form of communalism. This involves the use of sacred symbols, religious leaders, etc. (1+1+1)

28. Merits of Democracy are:

 (a) A democratic government is better form of government because it is more accountable form of government.

 (b) Democracy improves the quality of decision making.

 (c) Democracies give people a chance to become personally involved with their government: This is because the government is chosen by the people themselves.

 (d) A democracy encourages equality in a positive way: The structure of a democracy gives every vote an equal amount of weight during an election.

 (e) The structure of a democracy works to reduce issues with exploitation: All government formations are sensitive to exploitation because of the people who get elected into powerful positions.

 (f) Democracy allows people to collect their mistakes. $(1/2 \times 6)$

SECTION C

29. Congress reluctant in participation of women-

   (i)   Congress was keen only on the symbolic presence of women within the organization.

   (ii) Gandhi ji believed that role of women was to look after home and hearth so as being good mothers and good wives.

Participation of women in Civil Disobedience Movement

   i.   During Gandhiji's Salt March, lots of women came out to participate in protest marches.

   ii.   They manufactured salt and picketed liquor shops.

   iii. They boycotted foreign goods.

   iv.   Women were from high caste families and from rich peasant households participated.

   v.   Moved by Gandhiji's call, they began to see service to nation as a sacred duty of women.   (3)

30. The government can play a major role in making fair globalisation possible. Fair globalisation would create opportunities for all, and also ensure that benefits of globalisation are shared better. Government policies must protect the interests not only of the rich and the powerful, but also of all the people in the country.

   (i)   Government should ensure that labour laws are implemented and workers' rights are protected.

   (ii) Government should support small producers to improve their performance till the time they become strong enough to compete.

   (iii) If necessary, government should use trade and investment barriers.

   (iv) It can negotiate with WTO for fairer rules.

   (v)   It can also align with other developing countries with similar interests to fight against the domination of developed countries in the WTO.   (3)

31. "Democracy is seen to be good in principle but felt to be not so good in practice". The reasons for this are:

   (i)   In a democracy, people expect to have their **needs fulfilled** but it is not possible to look after everyone's needs as every country has **diverse culture and regions**. This often frustrates the common people.

   (ii) Ideally in a democracy everyone should be treated **equally** but there are instances where the minority opinion is not taken into account for a general view.

   (iii) Democracy is a people's government and it is imperative that people cast their **vote** to choose a government. But, many people skip the voting which does not serve the purpose of democracy.

 (iv) Regular elections may lead to **change in ruling party** and every party works in a different way. This may cause **instability**.

 (v) The people as well as the country will suffer if people are not **wise** enough in choosing a decent representative. (3)

32. The most abundantly available fossil fuel in India is **coal**. The different forms of coal are **Peat, Lignite, Bituminous** and **Anthracite**, let's talk about their importance in detail:

 (i) **Peat** : Decaying plants in swamps produce **peat** and it is burnt as fuel or applied to the soil to **improve the texture and moisture.**

 (ii) **Lignite:** It is **brown** is colour, soft and has high moisture content. **Generation of electricity** is the main usage of lignite.

 (iii) **Bituminous:** It's usually **black** in colour and has medium heat per kg. It is used for **producing coke.**

 (iv) **Anthracite:** The **carbon content in per kg is more than 90%** .It is used in **residential and commercial space heating.** (3)

OR

The two main categories in which communication divided into are **Personal communication and mass communication.**

Personal communication can be understood as **exchange of communication** in between two people.

The **Indian postal network is the largest in the world. It handles written communication** as well as **parcels**.

Mass communication **creates awareness** and **provides entertainment** among people about various national programmes and policies. It includes radio, television and newspaper, magazines, books and film. (3)

33. Rinderpest arrived in Africa in the late 1880s. Within two years, it spread in the whole continent. It affected the Africans in the following ways:

 (i) Rinderpest moved like forest fire in Africa.

 (ii) 90% of cattle were killed.

 (iii) The loss of cattle destroyed African livelihoods. Earlier people rarely worked for a wage. They possessed land and livestock. Due to Rinderpest, they were forced to work for wages and so it affected the economy.

 (iv) Colonial government forced the Africans into labour market. $(1 + 4 = 5)$

OR

Proto-industrialisation refers to the system of industries that existed in Europe before the arrival of modern machine run factories. Large scale industrial production took place for an international market. It was based in the countryside, not in factories.

Effects:

(i)   Open fields were disappearing and commons were being enclosed so common people had no alternative sources of income.

(ii) Many had small plots of land which could not provide work for all family members.

(iii) Merchants offered them advances for which they agreed.

(iv) They got a source of income which supplemented their shrinking income from cultivation.

$$(1 + 4 = 5)$$

34. Need to conserve mineral resources

(i)   Mineral resources are **limited** and **non-renewable**.

(ii) All minerals are **not evenly distributed** on the earth surface so it will take time to find all the minerals.

(iii) The **geological processes** of mineral formation are so **slow** but the **rate of consumption** is very **high**.

Mineral resources can be conserved by following ways:

(i)   There should be the **planned usage** of these resources.

(ii) **Bicycle or walk** through can be used as a mean of transport to travel short distances. **Judicious and proper use of** minerals should be promoted by government means like as **rebate in personal tax** for a person who use sustainable means for his transportation or other work .

(iii) **Switch off the vehicles automobiles** or engines at railway crossing or at a red traffic light.

(iv) The government **should implement some strict law** in order to conserve these resources.   (3)

Section D

35. (3 + 3)

  (a) (A) Ahmedabad

       (B) Calcutta

       (C) Champaran

  (b) (1) Kerala

       (2) Maharashtra

       (3) Durg

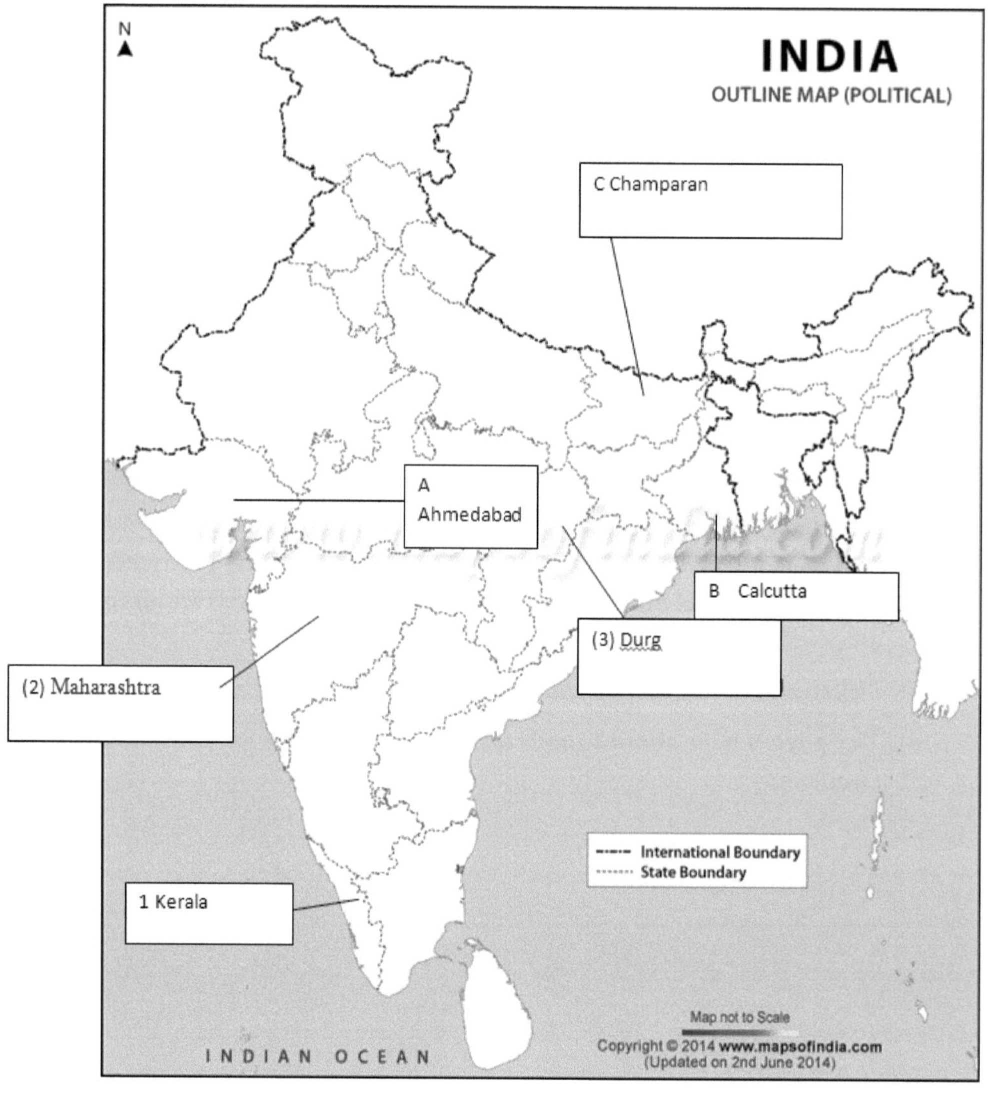

CBSE
Sample Question Paper 9

Social Science
Class X

Time : 3 hrs   **MM : 80**

General Instructions

  i. The question paper has **35** questions in all.

  ii. Marks are indicated against each question.

  iii. Questions from serial number **1** to **20** are objective type questions. Each question carries **one mark**. Answer them as instructed.

  iv. Questions from serial number **21** to **28** are **3 marks** questions. Answer of these questions should not exceed **80 words** each.

  v. Questions from serial number **29** to **34** are **5 marks** questions. Answer of these questions should not exceed **120 words** each.

  vi. Question number **35** is a map question of **6 marks** with two parts - **35 a.** from History (3 marks) and **35 b.** from Geography (3 marks).

SECTION A

1. The concept of _____________________emerged in Europe during the nineteenth century.   1

2. Power sharing helps in reducing conflict between ________________.   1

3. ___________________ consists of various proportions of sand, silt and clay.   1

4. In a SHG most of the decisions regarding savings and loan activities are taken by ___________________.   1

5. Textile industry is a __________ scale industry.   1

6. A government formed by the union of two or more political parties is called as
    ________________.   1

7. ________ is the official language of India.   1

8. Cargill Foods is an ________ MNC.   1

9. Who among the following hosted the Congress at Vienna in 1815?   1
    (i) Duke Metternich   (ii) Giuseppe Mazzini
    (iii)Napoleon   (iv) Otto Von Bismarck

10. The first cement plant in India was established at: 1
    (i) Maharashtra   (ii) Delhi
    (iii)Patna   (iv) Chennai

11. How many union territories are there in the Indian Federation?   1
    (i) 10   (ii) 7
    (iii)15   (iv) 17

12. One cannot refuse a payment made in rupees in India.   1

13. Bengaluru has emerged as the electronic capital of India.   1

14. World Trade Organisation aims to liberate international trade   1

15. Belgium is an example of 'coming together' federation.   1

16. Why did Gandhiji withdraw the Non-Cooperation Movement?   1

17. Name the first book printed by Johann Gutenberg?   1

18. Who is a feminist?   1

19. What is meant by the term Collateral?   1

20. What is foreign investment?   1

SECTION B

21. Sharing of powers makes a country more powerful and united. Justify the statement.   3

22. Name the national political party which gets inspiration from India's ancient culture and values. Mention four features of that party.   3

23. Describe the adverse effects of caste in politics in India.   3

24. "Agriculture and industry move hand in hand." Analyze the statement with three examples.   3

OR

Why is the air transport more popular in the north eastern part of the country? Give three reasons.   3

25. Why does disguised employment not help in the productivity of the country ? Explain with the help of example.   3

26. What was the civil code of 1804?   3

OR

Briefly describe Zollverein?

27. Explain the meaning of tertiary sector. Mention any two economic activities of this sector.   3

28. Enumerate the role of MNCs in the economic development of a country.   3

SECTION C

29. How can the formal sector loans be made beneficial for poor farmers and workers?   5

30. Write a note on Greek War of Independence.   5

31. How did Henry Ford revolutionize mass production in the U.S. ?   5

OR

What were the reasons for the decline of textile exports from India in the 19th century?

32. There is enough for everybody's need and not for anybody's greed .Explain this statement.   5

33. "Political parties are a necessary condition for a democracy". Analyze the statement with examples.   5

34. Write two important beverage crop of India .Explain the geographical conditions needed for its cultivation.   5

SECTION D

35. (a) Two items A and B are shown in the given political outline map of India. Identify these items with the help of information given below:

    (A)   The place which is known for Cotton Mill Workers Satyagraha.   1

    (B)   The place where the Non-Cooperation Movement was called off   1

On the same map, locate and label the following:

    (C) The place where Congress Session was held in September 1920.   1

(b) Two items (1) and (2) are shown in the given political outline map of India. Identify these items with the help of following information and write their correct names on the lines marked on the map.

    (1)   An iron and steel plant   1

    (2)   A nuclear power plant   1

On the same political map, locate and label the following:

    (3)   Vishakhapatnam   1

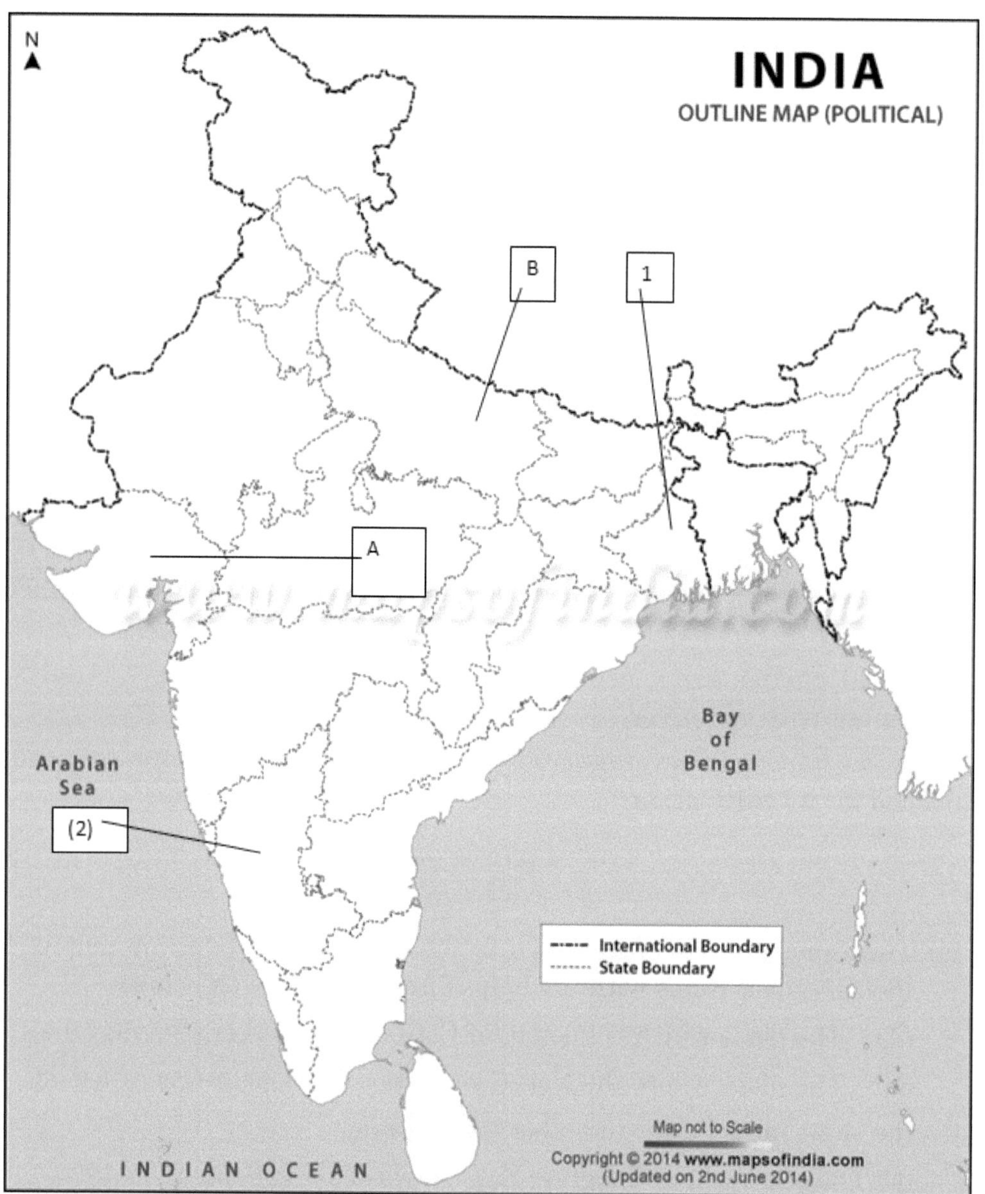

Solution

SECTION A

1. Nationalism
2. Diverse social groups
3. Alluvial soil
4. Members
5. Large (1)
6. Coalition (1)
7. Hindi (1)
8. American (1)
9. (i) Duke Metternich
10. (iv) Chennai
11. (ii) 7
12. True
13. True
14. True
15. False
16. Because the movement had turned violent. (1)
17. Bible (1)
18. A person who demands equal rights for women. (1)
19. It is an asset that the borrower owns and uses as a guarantee until the loan is repaid to the lender. (1)
20. Investment made by MNCs is called foreign investment. (1)

SECTION B

21. 1. power sharing ensures the maximum participation of peoples, which ensures the stability of government .

    2. power sharing accommodates diverse groups. It helps to reduce the possibility of conflicts between different social group which ensure peace in nation.

    3. it ensures the people participation which creates a sense of responsibility in citizens. (3)

22. The national political party which gets inspiration from India's ancient culture and values **is Bharatiya Janata Party, founded in 1980** by reviving the previous **Bharatiya Jana Sangh.**

Four features of BJP are as follows:

(1) A **uniform civil code** was promoted for people living in the country, irrespective of different castes and religion and have put ban on religious conversions.

(2) The party wants to add complete state of **Jammu and Kashmir** to be **integrated** with India **(both politically and territorially).**

(3) Being **cultural nationalism** an important element of its conception of Indian nationhood and politics, BJP wants to build modern and strong India. (3)

23. There can be several adverse effects of caste in politics in India:

1. People prefer **vote the candidate of their caste** in elections rather than voting a right person who would hold the responsibilities properly.

2. Inclusion of caste in politics **leads to disparities and social violence.**

3. It leads **to disintegration of people and societies** of a country on the basis of caste and religion.

4. Many times the rightful heir of a post does not get a chance **because of reservations** (3)

24. Below are the ways which justify that agriculture and industry move hand in hand:

(1) **Transportation** provided by different industries to import raw materials from fields to different places or also helps bring finished goods to the market.

(2) **Excess Labour** in agriculture sectors are employed by industrial sector.

(3) **Agricultural produced raw materials** are processed in the industries. For example, cotton used to produce textile. (3)

OR

Air transport is more popular in north eastern part of india because of

1. Dissected relief features.

2. Frequent floods.

3. Presence of dense forests. (3)

25. Disguised unemployment does not help to enhance the productivity of the country because these additional workers are acctually not required for the work, without they being there the productivity would be the same. we can take example of rural family having eight member, who involves in ration shops. If the one person remove from this shop the business output will be same

26. The civil code of 1804 usually known as the Napoleonic code which abolished all the privileges based on birth, created quality before the law and secured the right to property . (3)

OR

In 1834, Zollverein or customs union was established at the initiative of Prussia and joined by the most of the German states. The union did away with tariff barriers and decreased the number of currencies from over thirty to only two .   (3)

27. Tertiary sectors involves all those activities that help in the development of the primary and secondary sectors. These activities, by themselves, do not produce a good but they are an aid or support for the production process. It is also known as Service sector.

    Two economic activities of this sector are-banking, transport, storage, communication, etc.
                                                                (Any two)   (2+1)

28. Role of MNCs in the economic development:

    (i)   MNCs place order for production with small producers: Due to this small producers are able to get a global exposure as well as a huge customer base.

    (ii) MNCs are setting up partnerships with local companies: The local companies are able to expand themselves at a global level.

    (iii) They are interlinking markets all over the world: Interlinking of markets all over the world has led to the exchange of foreign currency and thereby providing a boom to the economy of various countries.   (1+1+1)

Section C

29. Formal sector loans can be made beneficial for poor farmers and workers in the following ways :

    (i)   Create awareness to farmers about formal sector loans.

    (ii) Process of providing loans should be made easier. It should be simple, fast and timely.

    (iii) More number of Nationalized Banks/Cooperative Banks should be opened in the rural sector.

    (iv) Banks and cooperatives should increase facility of providing loans so that dependence on informal sources of credit reduces.

    (v)   The benefits of loans should be extended to poor farmers and small scale industries.

    (vi) While formal sector loans need to expand, it is also necessary that everyone receives these loans.   (Any five) (1 × 5 = 5)

30. (i)   Greece had been a part of the Ottoman Empire since the 15th century. Struggle for independence began in 1821.

    (ii) Greece got support from Greeks living in exile and West-Europeans who had sympathies for ancient Greek culture.

    (iii) Literary artists lauded Greece as the cradle of European civilisation and mobilised public opinion to support its fight against Muslim empire.

(iv) English poet Lord Byron, organised funds, fought in war and died of fever in 1824.

(v) Finally, The treaty of Constantinople of 1832 recognized Greece as an independent nation.

31. (i) Henry Ford adapted the assembly line of a Chicago slaughter house to his new car plant in Detroit.

(ii) The assembly line allowed a faster and cheaper way of producing vehicles. It forced workers to repeat a single task mechanically and continuously.

(iii) This increased their efficiency in the single task and the speed of production too.

(iv) Standing in front of the conveyor belt, no worker could delay the motions or take a break.

(v) In the beginning, many workers quit, since they could not cope up with the stress of work. Henry Ford doubled their wages and against that, he not only increased the speed of the production time but also banned trade unions from operating in his plants.

(1+1+1+1+1)

OR

Following were the reasons for the decline of textile exports from India in the 19th century:

(i) Britain imposed import duties on cotton textiles, thus export market got declined.

(ii) Exports of British goods to India increased. The Manchester goods flooded Indian markets.

(iii) The machine-made goods were cheaper and weavers could not compete with them.

(iv) Raw cotton exports from India to Britain shot up the prices of cotton.

(v) By 1850, exports from most weaving regions got declined and desolated.

(1+1+1+1+1)

32. The statement of Gandhi ji has a great meaning regarding resources. We can understand this by following points-

1. it means that the earth has abundant resources to satisfy everyone's needs but in our greed and hurry to develop. We have been exploiting our resources recklessly.

2. On the name of development we have indulged in activities like deforestation, overgrazing, encroachment into forest lands, overuse of ground water, use of plastics.

3. The exploitation of natural resources not only harms the environment but many cripple the future generations of the development itself.

So we should accept the sustainable development to uphold our earth   (5)

33. "Political parties are a necessary condition for a democracy".

The importance of political party is **directly linked to the emergence** of representative democracies.

As societies became **large and complex**, they also needed some agency to gather different views on various issues and to present these to the government.

They needed some ways, to bring various representatives together so that a responsible government could be formed.

They needed a **mechanism** to support or restrain the government, make policies, justify or oppose them.

Political parties **fulfill** these needs that every representative. (5)

34. Two most important beverage crops of India are

(i)   Tea and

(ii) Coffee.

Tea :

Temperature — 20° to 30°C

Rainfall — 150 to 200 cms.

Soil — Well drained soils

Labour — Cheap, abundant and skilled labour

Areas — Assam, West Bengal, Tamil Nadu and Kerala

Coffee:

Temperature - 15°C to 28°C

Rainfall — 150 to 200 cms.

Soil — Rich, well drained, loamy soil

Labour — Cheap labour is essential

Areas — Hills around Nilgiris, Karnataka, Kerala and Tamil Nadu (3)

SECTION D

35. (3 + 3)

- (a) (A) Ahmedabad
  - (B) Chauri Chaura
  - (C) Calcutta
- (b) (1) Durgapur
  - (2) Kaiga
  - (3) Vishakhapatanam

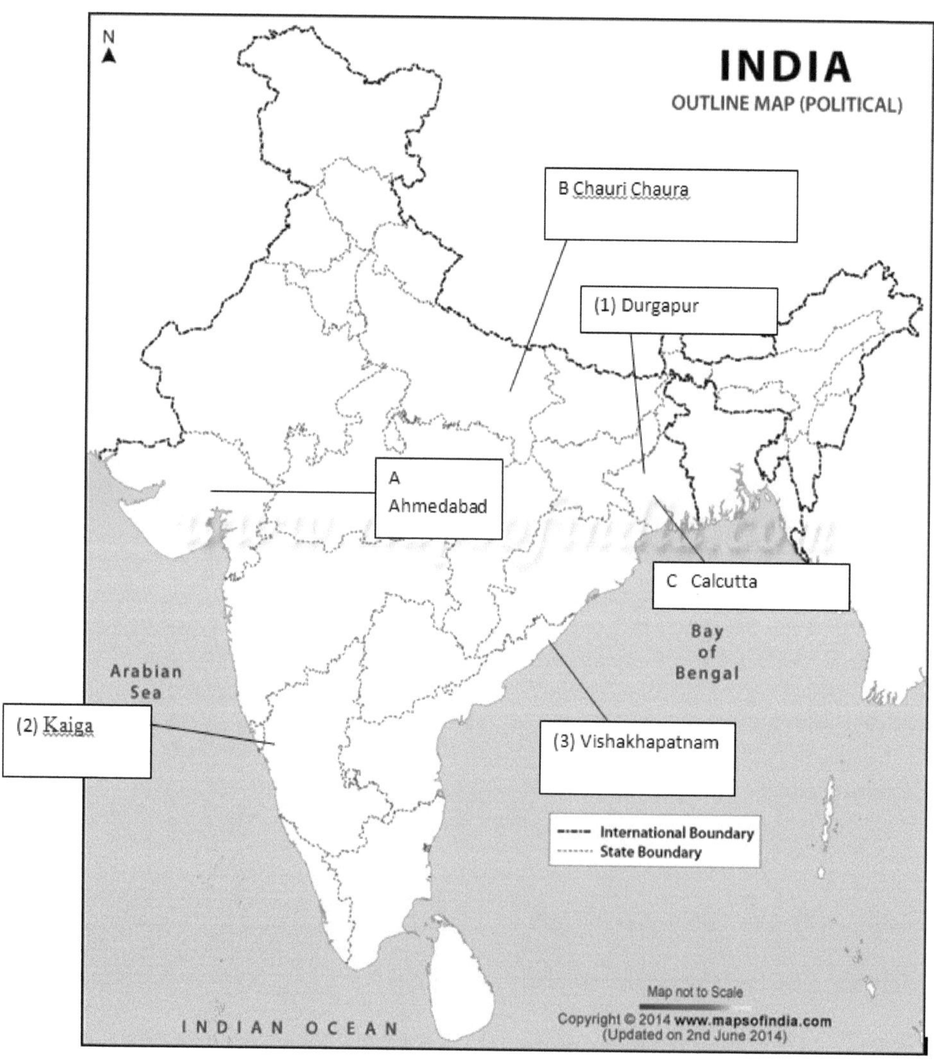

CBSE
Sample Question Paper 10

Social Science
Class X

Time : 3 hrs	MM : 80

General Instructions

i. The question paper has **35** questions in all.

ii. Marks are indicated against each question.

iii. Questions from serial number **1** to **20** are objective type questions. Each question carries **one mark**. Answer them as instructed.

iv. Questions from serial number **21** to **28** are **3 marks** questions. Answer of these questions should not exceed **80 words** each.

v. Questions from serial number **29** to **34** are **5 marks** questions. Answer of these questions should not exceed **120 words** each.

vi. Question number **35** is a map question of **6 marks** with two parts - **35 a.** from History (3 marks) and **35 b.** from Geography (3 marks).

SECTION A

1. 'Hind Swaraj' was written by___________________.   1

2. The subject of adoption falls under __________ list.   1

3. Industries which are owned and operated by government agencies are called as ___________.   1

4. Production of a commodity, mostly through the natural process, is an activity in _______ sector.   1

5. _________ is the most important mode of transport in India.   1

6. _______________ protects the federal structure of the country.   1

7. Decentralisation in India happened in the year _______________.   1

8. Economic survey is the subject matter of Ministry of _______________.   1

9. What was the prime purpose of the Civil Disobedience Movement?   1
   (i) Poorna Swaraj
   (ii) Liberation of princely states
   (iii)Abolition of Sati
   (iv)Abolition of Salt law

10. Which of the two steel plants are in collaboration with Russia?   1
    (i) Bhadravati and Salem
    (ii) Bhilai and Bokaro
    (iii)Bokaro and Jamshedpur
    (iv)Burnpur and Durgapur

11. Which community is in majority in Sri Lanka?   1
    (i) Below poverty line group
    (ii) Hindi speaking
    (iii)Sinhala-speaking community
    (iv)None of the above

12. Workers in the tertiary sector do not produce goods   1

13. The air transport was nationalised in 1990.   1

14. Rapid improvement in technology has been one major factor that has stimulated
    the globalisation process.   1

15. Vertical distribution of power results in a balance of power among various
    institutions.   1

16. Where did the Frankfurt Assembly convene?   1

17. Who formed the secret society named 'Young Italy'?   1

18. What is meant by an accountable government?   1

19. What is the full form of HDI ?   1

20. Which is India's most progressive state in terms of education, literacy and
    health.   1

Section B

21. Describe the role of Giuseppe Mazzini as an Italian revolutionary.   3

OR

Name the female allegory who represents France. Describe her main
characteristics.

22. Indiscriminate use of resources has led to numerous problems." Justify the statement. 3

OR

Write the geographical condition needed for cultivation of Zaid with location.

23. Distinguish between Holding together and Coming together Federations. 3

24. Explain the type of Power sharing in India. 3

25. What were the special elements of the Belgian model? 3

26. Write the function of UNDP. Write the criteria used to publish HDR. 3

27. Distinguish between formal and informal sources of credit. 3

28. Explain the factors that have enabled Globalisation with a example. 3

SECTION C

29. The function and shape of the family were completely transformed by life in the industrial city Clarify the statement with regard to urbanization that happened in England. 5

OR

Explain the negative aspects of globalization in Africa.

30. Examine role of Gandhi ji in the Indian national movement. 5

31. Classify industries on the basis of ownership and investment. 5

32. Mention any two inland waterways of India. Write three characteristics of each. 5

33. Describe "It is very difficult to reform politics through legal ways". Evaluate the statement. 5

34. How do banks play an important role in the economy of India? Explain. 5

SECTION D

35. (a) Two items A and B are shown in the given political outline map of India. Identify these items with the help of information given below:

    (A) The place associated with Peasant Satyagraha   1

    (B) The place where Congress Session was held in 1927.   1

  On the same map, locate and label the following:

    (C) Chauri Chaura   1

  (b) Two items (1) and (2) are shown in the given political outline map of India. Identify these items with the help of following information and write their correct names on the lines marked on the map.

    (1) An iron ore mine   1

    (2) An oil field   1

On the same political map, locate and label the following:

(3)   Bangalore   1

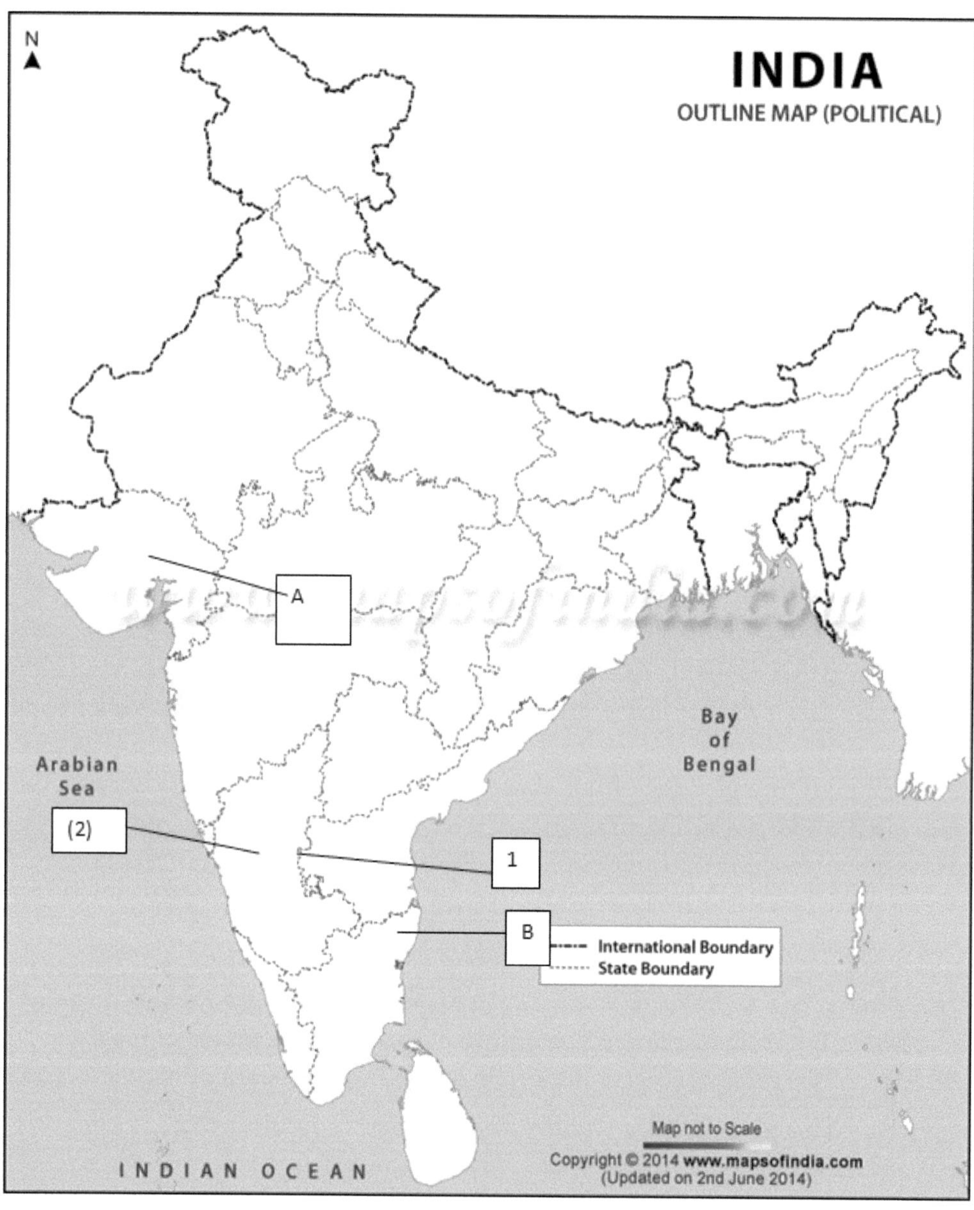

Solution

SECTION A

1. Mahatma Gandhi (1)
2. concurrent list (1)
3. Public Sector Industries (1)
4. Primary (1)
5. Railways (1)
6. Judiciary (1)
7. 1992 (1)
8. Finance (1)
9. (iv) Abolition of Salt law (1)
10. (ii) Bhilai and Bokaro (1)
11. (iii) Sinhala-speaking community (1)
12. True (1)
13. True (1)
14. True (1)
15. False (1)
16. At the church of St. Paul (1)
17. Giuseppe Mazzini (1)
18. In an accountable government, people have the right to elect the leaders to form a government. (1)
19. Human Development Index. (1)
20. Kerala (1)

SECTION B

21. The role of Giuseppe Mazzini as an Italian revolutionary:

    (a) He founded two secret societies named Young Italy in Marseilles and Young Europe in Berne.

    (b) Members of these societies were like-minded young men from Poland, France, Italy and German states.

    (c) Mazzini's relentless opposition to monarchy and his vision of democratic republic frightened the conservatives. (1+1+1)

OR

Marianne was the female allegory who represented France.

Her characteristics were drawn from:

(i)   Those of liberty and republic.

(ii) These were the red cap, the tricolor, the cockade.

(iii) Statues of Marianne were erected in public squares to remind the public of the national symbol of unity and to persuade them to identify with it.

(iv) Her images were marked on coins and stamps of 1850.   (Any three) $(1 \times 3 = 3)$

22. Indiscriminate use of resources had led to numerous problems like :-

(i)   **Depletion of resources** for satisfying the interest of a few people.

(ii) **Division of society** into rich and poor by accumulation of resources in the hands of few individuals.

(iii) Global ecological crisis like global warming, depletion of ozone layer, environmental pollution and land degradation.   (3)

OR

These crops are mainly grown in the summer season during a period called the "Zaid crop season." They require warm dry weather for major growth period and longer day length for flowering. The main produce are seasonal fruits and vegetables they are sown during the months of March and harvested by June., watermelon, pumpkin etc are the main crop.   (3)

23. Coming together federation-

Independent states come together to form a bigger unit, all the constituent states usually have a equal power. USA, Switzerland and Australia having the coming together federation

Holding together federation-

A large geographical country split its power between states and national government.

Central government exercise more power. India, Spain, and Belgium   (3)

24. In india we have two type of power sharing

1.   Horizontal – power is divided among organs of government, i.e – legislative, executive and judiciary.

2.   Power is shared among the different levels of the governments. Power involves the highest and the lower levels of government. The lower organs work under the higher organs.   (3)

25. The special elements of the Belgian model are distinguished as following:

1.   There were equal numbers of French and Dutch speaking ministers in the central government so that no single community has the privilege of making unilateral decisions.

2. The powers of central and state government were shared so that states are not subordinate to the centre.

3. There was **a separate government** for Brussels having equal representation of both the communities.

4. The Belgian model introduced a third form of government known as the **community government** which is elected by the people belonging **to one language** community. (3)

26. To **encourage global development**, UNDP focuses on poverty reduction, HIV/AIDS, democratic governance, **energy** and environment, social development, and crisis prevention and recovery.

Per capita income, literacy rate, infant mortality rate is use to publish HDR report.) (3)

27. Formal sources:

(i) They follow those sources of credit, which are registered by the government and have to follow its rules and regulations.

(ii) RBI supervises the functioning of formal sources of credit.

(iii) They generally charge lower rates of interest.

(iv) Their main motive is social welfare.

Example: Banks and cooperatives.

Informal sources:

(i) These include those small and scattered units which are largely outside the control of the government.

(ii) There is no organisation which supervises the credit activities.

(iii) They charge much higher rates of interest.

(iv) Their main motive is profit-making.

Example: Moneylenders, traders, employees, relatives and friends, etc (3)

28. The some important factor that have enabled Globalisation -

(1) Economy:

The cost of goods and values to the end user determine the movement of goods and value addition. The overall economics of a particular industry or trade is an important factor in globalisation.

(2) Resources and Markets:

The natural resources like minerals, coal, oil, gas, human resources, water, etc. make an important contribution in globalisation.

(3) Industrial Organisation:

The technological development in the areas of production, product mix and firms are helping organisations to expand their operations. The hiring of services and procurement of sub-assemblies and components have a strong influence in the globalisation process. (3)

SECTION C

29. a. Ties between members of households loosened, and among the working class the institution of marriage tended to break down.

b. Women of the upper and middle classes in Britain, on the other hand, faced increasingly higher levels of isolation, although their lives were made easier by domestic maids who cooked, cleaned and cared for young children on low wages.

c. Women who worked for wages had some control over their lives, particularly among the lower social classes. However, many social reformers felt that the family as an institution had broken down, and needed to be saved or reconstructed by pushing these women back into the home.

d. The city encouraged a new spirit of individualism among both men and women, and a freedom from the collective values that were a feature of the smaller rural communities.

e. But men and women did not have equal access to this new urban space. As women lost their industrial jobs and conservative people railed against their presence in public spaces, women were forced to withdraw into their homes.   (5)

30. (i) Gandhiji lived a simple life. His life was his message. He was like a Sanyasi.

(ii) Gandhiji introduced a powerful method of struggle called Satyagraha. This non violent method attracted common people in to the National Movement.

(iii) Gandhiji made social reform a part of the National Movement. He fought against untouchability.

(iv) He supported Hindu – Muslim unity. Under his leadership Hindus and Muslims fought together against the British.

(v) He launched powerful mass movements like Non Co Operation Movement, Civil Disobedience Movement and Quit India Movement.   (5)

31. On the basis of ownership, industries can be classified as-

Public Sector: These industries are aimed and operated by the government agencies.

Private Sector: These industries are owned and operated by private entrepreneurs, e.g., TISCO, Bajaj Auto Ltd., Reliance Industries, Dabur Industries, etc.

Joint Sector: These industries are jointly run by the state and individual or a group of individuals. Oil India Ltd (OIL) is jointly owned by public and private sectors.

Cooperative Sector: These industries are owned and operated by the producers or suppliers of raw materials, workers or both. They pool in the resources and share the profits or losses proportionately such as the sugar industry in Maharashtra, the coir in dustry in Kerala.

On the basis of investment industries can be classified as-

   (i) **Small-scale Industries:** A small scale industry is defined with reference to the maximum investment allowed on the assets of a unit. This limit has changed over a period of time. At present the maximum investment allowed is rupees one crore.

   (ii) **Large-scale Industries:** If investment is more than one crore on any industry then it is known as a large-scale industry. (5)

32. Two inland waterways of India are:

   (i) **The Brahmaputra River** between Sadiya and Dhubri.

   (ii) **The Ganga River** between Allahabad and Haldia.

Three characteristics of The Brahmaputra River between Sadiya and Dhubri are:

   (i) It is also known as **National Waterway 2.**

   (ii) Its **length** is **891 km.**

   (iii) It facilitates **national security** and is used as transportation **link between states.**

Three characteristics of The Ganga River between Allahabad and Haldia:

   (i) It is known as **National Waterway 1.**

   (ii) It is **1,620 km** long.

   (iii) It provides **pilgrimage.** (5)

33. Practice of wrong political practices can be discouraged by carefully **implying new laws** but the challenge to democracy is that **these changes are not enough to reform the politics.** Thinking of legal ways of **reforming politics** is very tempting because new **laws can ban undesirable things.** Law plays an **important** role in political reform. **For example,** in cricket, changes in rules of the game are not enough to improve the quality of the game but mainly it **depends on administration, coaches and players.** In the similar way, political reformation depends on **political parties, activists, movements.** Sometimes the result of these changes is **counter-productive.** For example, people with more than two children have been **banned** from contesting panchayat elections that restricted many poor women and men to take part in the election. As it is the **denial** of the democratic opportunity but it was not intended. So we can say **"It is very difficult to reform politics through legal ways".** (5)

34. (i) Banks provide **credit at cheap and affordable rates** to the **poor.**

   (ii) **Banks accepts the deposits** and also pays an **amount as interest on the deposits.**

   (iii) Bank uses a major portion of the **deposits to give loans.**

   (iv) Banks helps in establishment of **large scale industries** which **brings foreign exchange,** and thus adding to the **national income of the country.**

   (v) **Provides employment and growth opportunities** to the **low income group.** (5)

Section D

35. (3 + 3)

   (I) (A) Kheda

         (B) Madras

         (C) Chauri Chaura

  (II) (1) Bellary

         (2) Digboi

         (3) Bangalore

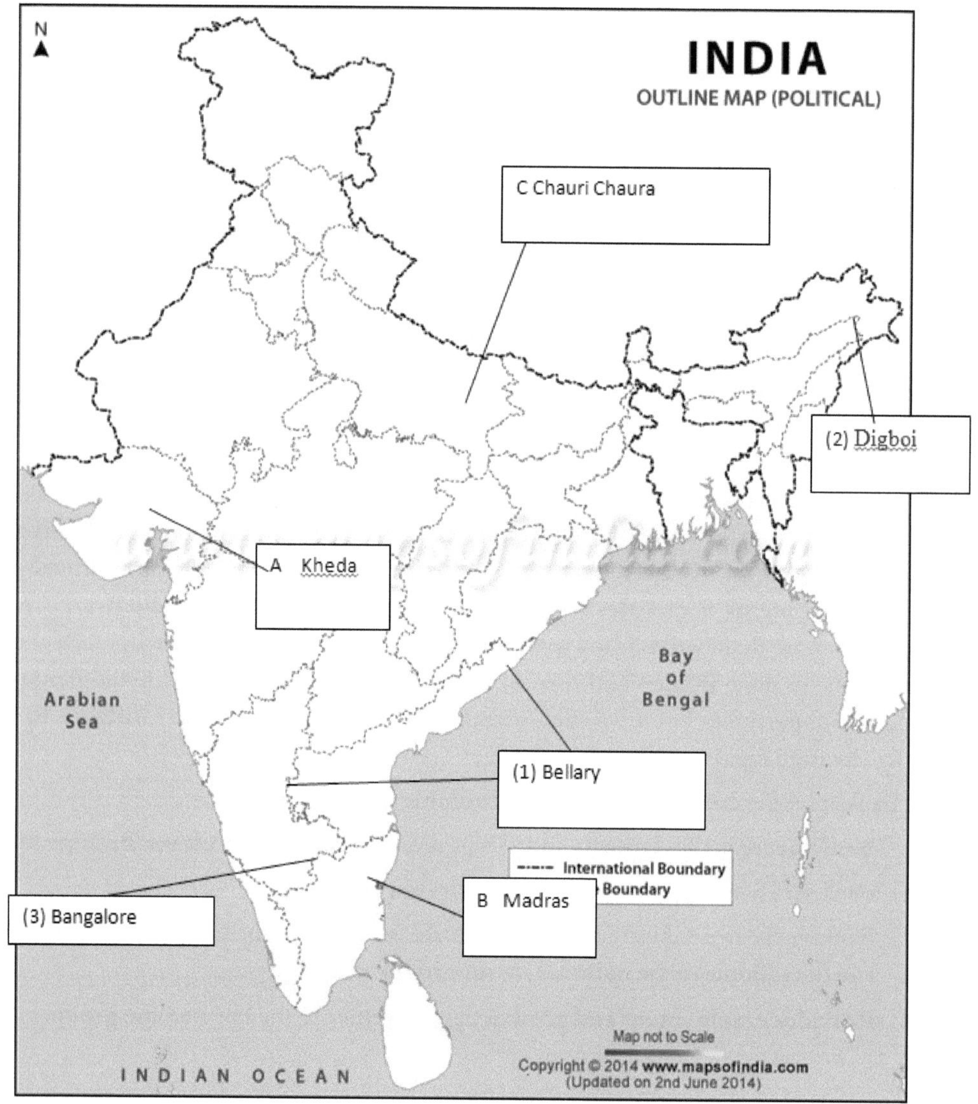

CBSE
Solved Paper 2019

Social Science
Class X

Time : 3 hrs	MM : 80

(i) The question paper is divided into four sections – Section A, Section B, Section C and Section D.

(ii) The question paper has **26** questions in all.

(iii) All questions are **compulsory**.

(iv) Marks are indicated against each question.

(v) Questions from serial number **1** to **7** are very short answer type questions. Each question carries **one mark.**

(vi) Questions from serial number **8** to **18** are **3 marks** questions. Answer of these questions should not exceed **80 words** each.

(vii) Questions from serial number **19** to **25** are **5 marks** questions. Answers of these questions should not exceed **100 words** each.

(viii) Question number **26** is a map question. It has **5 marks** with two parts **26(A)** and **26(B)**. **26(A)** from History (**2 marks**) and **26(B)** from Geography (**3 marks**). After completion attach the map inside your answer book.

Section A

1. How had hand printing technology introduced in Japan? (1)

OR

How had translation process of novels into regional languages helped to spread their popularity?

2. Interpret the contribution of French in the economic development of Mekong delta region. (1)

OR

Interpret the concept of 'liberalisation' in the field of economic sphere during the nineteenth century in Europe.

3. What may be a goal of landless rural labourers regarding their income? (1)

OR

What may be a goal of prosperous farmer of Punjab.

4. How can democratic reforms be carried out by political parties? (1)

5. How is over–irrigation responsible for land degradation in Punjab? (1)

OR

How is cement industry responsible for land degradation?

6. Distinguish between 'primary' and secondary sectors. (1)

7. Explain the importance of formal sector loans in India. (1)

Section B

8. Describe any three main features of 'Rabi crop season'. (3)

OR

Describe any three main features of 'Kharif crop season'.

9. How had Napoleonic code exported to the regions under French control? Explain with examples. (3)

OR

Explain with examples three barriers that are responsible to economic growth in Vietnam.

10. How had the Imperial State in China been the major producer of printed material for a long time? Explain with examples (3)

OR

How had novels been easily available to the masses in Europe during nineteenth century? Explain with examples.

11. Analyse the impact of 'water scarcity'. (3)

12. "Consequences of environmental degradation do not respect national or state boundaries" Justify the statement (3)

13. Why is the 'tertiary sector' becoming important in India? Explain any three reasons. (3)

OR

How do we count various goods and services for calculating gross domestic product (G.D.P) of a country? Explain with example.

14. Explain any three functions of opposition political parties. (3)

15. How can consumers use their 'Right to seek redressal' Explain with example. (3)

16. "The assertion of social diversities in a democratic country is very normal and can be healthy" Justify the statement with arguments. (3)

OR

"Social divisions affect politics" Examine the statement.

17. "Women still lag much behind men in India despite some improvements since independence" Analyse the statement. (3)

18. Describe the importance of formal sources of credit in the economic development. (3)

OR

Describe the bad effects of informal sources of credit on borrowers.

SECTION C

19. "Roadways still have an edge over railways in India." Support the statement with example. $(5 \times 1 = 5)$

20. Compare the situation of Belgium and Sri Lanka considering their location, size and cultural aspects. $(1 + 1 + 3 = 5)$

OR

How is the idea of power sharing emerged? Explain different forms that have common arrangements of power sharing.

21. Explain five types of 'Industrial pollution'. (5)

22. Who had organized the Dalits into the 'Depressed classes Association' in 1930? Describe his achievements.

OR   (5)

Define the term 'Civil Disobedience Movement'. Describe the participation of rich and poor peasant communities in the 'Civil Disobedience Movement'

23. "Indian trade had played a crucial role in the late nineteenth century world economy" Analyze the statement. $(5 \times 1 = 5)$

OR

"Series of changes affected the pattern of industrialization in India by the early twentieth century" Analyze the statement.

OR

"Industrialization had changed the form of urbanization in the modern period." Analyze the statement with special reference of London.

24. Describe any five factors that make democracy is a better form of government than other alternatives. $(5 \times 1 = 5)$

25. Explain any five facilities available in the special economic zones developed by the Central and State Governments to attract foreign investment. $(5 \times 1 = 5)$

Section D

26. **(A)** Two features A and B are marked on the given political outline map of India. Identify these features with the help of the following information and write their correct names on the lines marked near them. $(1 \times 2 = 2)$

   (a) The place where the Indian National Congress Session was held.

   (b) The city where Jallianwalla Bagh incident took place.

(B) Locate and lanel any three of the following with appropriate symbols on the same given outline political map of India. $(1 \times 3 = 3)$

   (i)   Kalpakkam   –   Nuclear Power Plant
   (ii) Vijayanagar   –   Iron and Steel Plant
   (iii) Noida   –   Software Technology Park
   (iv) Paradeep   –   Sea Port
   (v)   Sardar Sarovar   –   Dam

Solution

SECTION A

1. Buddhist missionaries from China introduced hand-printing technology into Japan around AD 768-770. The oldest Japanese book, printed in AD 868, is the Buddhist 'Diamond Sutra'. Containg six sheets of text and woodcut illustrations. Pictures were printed on textiles, playing cards and paper money which made publishing very interesting. (1)

OR

English novels translated into regional Indian languages were initially not very popular as the Indian people could not relate the stories and characters to their own lives. But translation process of novels bring different spoken languages of people closer. These novels produce the sense of a shared world between diverse people in a nation. Novels also bring understanding of different cultures and values. (1)

2. The French began by building canals and draining lands in the Mekong delta to increase cultivation to bring about economic development. They used labour for construction of irrigation facilities to improve rice cultivation, built infrastructure and transportation facilities for the export of agricultural produce. (1)

OR

The term 'liberalism' is derived from the Latin word 'liber' means free. In the economic sphere. liberalism stood for the freedom of markets and the abolition of state–imposed restrictions on the movement of goods and capital. (1)

3. Development goals for, landless rural labourers regarding their income would be: (1)

   (i) To get more days of work and better wages.

   (ii) To get quality education for their children.

   (iii) No social discrimination

OR

Development goals for prosperous farmers of Punjab would be (1)

   (i) Low price of food grains.

   (ii) Assured high family income through higher support prices for their crops.

   (iii) Hardworking and cheap labourers.

4. Political parties need to have strong internal democracy, avoid dynastic succession, money and muscle power and by offering meaningful choice to the voters which could lead to democratic reforms. (1)

5. Water is very important for the growth of plant but excessive irrigation of field leads to water logging of soil. Therefore, over–irrigation is responsible for land degradation due to water–logging which leads to increase in salinity and alkalinity in the soil. (1)

OR

Excessive mining of limestone, silica and gypsum which are used as raw material for cement industry leads to land degradation. It later on settles down in the surrounding areas, affecting infiltration of water and crop cultivation. (1)

6. **Primary Sectors:** The primary sector is also called agriculture sector. It constitutes the backbone of our economy and the major sources of employment. Primary activity which is involved with the production or extraction of natural resources. (1/2)

    Secondary Sectors: Secondary sector involves use of natural goods and transform them into something more valuable by the manufacturing process. It is also called industrial sector. (1/2)

7. Importance of formal sector loans in India:

    (i)   The rate of interest charged on formal sector is lower than of informal sources of credit.

    (1/2)

    (ii)   Reserve Bank of India supervises their function. (1/2)

SECTION B

8. There are three main features of 'Rabi crop reason'

    (i)   Rabi crops are grown in winter from October to December and harvested in summer from April to June. (1)

    (ii)   Some Rabi crops are wheat, barley, peas, gram and mustard. (1)

    (iii)   These crops are grown in large parts of India such as Punjab, Haryana and Himachal Pradesh etc. (1)

OR

There are three main features of 'Kharif crop season'

    (i)   Kharif crops are grown with the onset of monsoon and harvested in September–October. (1)

    (ii)   Some important crops are paddy. maize, jowar, bajra, toor, moong, urad, cotton etc. (1)

    (iii)   Rice is an important Kharif crop. Some important rice growing regions are Assam, West Bengal, Coastal region of Odisha, Andhra Pradesh, Tamilnadu etc. (1)

9. The civil code of 1804, known as the Napoleonic code.

    These codes were the revolutionary principles of administration and were exported to the regions under French control. (1)

    For example, in the Dutch Republic in Switzerland, Italy and Germany. Napoleon simplified administrative divisive, abolished the feudal system and freed peasants from serfdom and manorial dues. (1)

    Peasants, workers and new businessman enjoyed a new–found freedom. Businessmen and small–scale producers of goods in particular, began to realise that uniform laws, standardised weights and measures and a common national currency would facilitate the movement and exchange of goods and capital from one region to another. (1)

OR

According to an influential writer and policy–maker Paul Bernard, several barriers to economic growth in Vietnam such as:

(i) High population level in Vietnam proved to be and obstacle to economic growth. (1)

(ii) Low agricultural productivity was another barrier that hindered the economic growth. (1)

(iii) Excessive indebtedness among the peasants that did not promote economic growth in Vietnam. (1)

(iv) The French colonialists did little to industrialise Vietnam and in the rural areas, landlordism spread and the standard of living declined. (1)

10. The earliest print technique developed in China. The imperial state in China was a large bureaucratic system, that sponsored the printing technique by the way of conducting examinations. China possessed a huge bureaucratic system which recruited its personnel through civil service examinations. Textbooks for this examination were printed in vast numbers under the sponsorship of the imperial state. (2)

From the sixteenth century. the number of examinations candidates went up and that increased the volume of print which node the Imperial state in China a major producer of printed material for a long time. (1)

OR

The Novel was one of the first mass–produced items to be sold in Europe. Novels created a sense of belonging on the basis of ones language. They dealt with the life of common people and they were cheap. Publishing markets helped in more sell and production of novels which was available to the masses in Europe during nineteenth century. (2)

Technological improvements in printing brought down the price of books and innovations in marketing led to expanded sale. In France, publishers found that they could make super profits by hiring out novels by the hour. (1)

11. Water is an essential resource for humans. Water scarcity is indeed the outcome of large and growing population. Humans require water for their various activities and more the number of people more the consumption. Water scarcity may lead to following impacts:

(i) Ground water level will decline. (1)

(ii) It may adversely affect water availability that shall impact agriculture and industry. (1)

(iii) Food grain production will be affected which may affect food security of the country. (1)

12. It is true that environmental degradation do not respect national or state boundaries. It has international and global affects because our future is linked together through common environmental and ecological system. Global warming, acid rain etc are the issues that cannot be tackled by one nation. It is a global concern. (2)

For example, if Indian Thermal power plants are causing massive air pollution, it affects our neighbouring countries like Pakistan, Bangladesh, Sri Lanka and others as well. Similarly, deforestation in Brazil has caused disturbance in rainfall pattern throughout South America. (1)

13. Importance of Tertiary Sector in India:

   (i) In any country, several services such as hospitals, educational institutions, post and telegraph services, defence, transport, banks etc, are required. These can be considered as basic services. (1)

   (ii) In development of agriculture and industry leads to the development of services such as transport, trade, storage etc. Greater the development of the primary and secondary sectors, more would be the demand for such services. (1)

   (iii) With the increase in income levels, certain sections of people start demanding many more services like tourism better educational facilities, communication services etc thereby, giving a boost to the tertiary sector. (1)

OR

The various goods and services are counted on the basis of the value of each goods or services, not on the basis of actual numbers.

   (i) The value of final goods and services produced in each sector during a particular year provides the total production of the sector for that year. The sum of all the three sector's production within a country is known as Gross Domestic Product (G.D.P) of a country. (1½)

   (ii) For example, a farmer sells wheat to a flour mill for ₹ 18/kg. The mill grinds the wheat and sells the flour to a biscuit company for ₹ 20/ kg. The biscuit company uses flour, sugar and oil to make the packets of biscuits. It sells biscuits in the market ₹ 45/ packet. Now, biscuits are the final goods. So, only the value of all final goods and services produced within a country during a particular year is counted as GDP. (1½)

14. Those parties that lose in the elections play the role of opposition to the parties in power. There are three functions of opposition political parties:

   (i) By voicing different views and criticizing government for its failures of programmes and wrong policies and their implementation. (1)

   (ii) It keeps people aware of wrong policies and programmes of the government. (1)

   (iii) It provides alternatives to choose from as it voices those views which are different from the party in power and helpful for the peoples of that country. (1)

15. Right to Seek Redressal : Consumers have the right to seek redressal against unfair trade practices and exploitation. If any damage is done to a consumer, he or she has the right to get a compensation depending on the degree of damage. There is a need to provide an easy and effective public system by which this can be done. (2)

For example, Deepak had sent a money order to his village for his daughter's marriage. The money did not reach to his daughter at the time when she needed it nor did it reach month's later. Therefore, Deepak can filed a case in the district level consumer court and exercised right to seek redressal. (1)

16. Social diversities in a democratic country is very normal and healthy. It divides similar people from one another but also unite very different people belonging to different social groups. (1)

The assertion of social diversities in a country does not require to be seen as a source of danger.

(i) In a democracy, political expression of social divisions is very normal and can be healthy. This allows different disadvantaged and marginal social groups to express their grievances and get the government to attend these. (1)

(ii) This leads to strengthening of a democracy. People who feel marginalized, deprived and discriminated, have to fight against the injustices. Such a fight often takes the democratic path, voicing their demands in a peaceful and constitutional manner and seeking a fair position through elections. (1)

OR

All social differences and diversities do not lead to social divisions. A combination of social divisions and politics can be really dangerous. A democracy involves competition among various political parties. The cases of Sri Lanka and Yugoslavia are clear examples.

While political competition along religious and ethnic lines led to the disintegration of Yugoslavia into six independent countries, the situation in Sri Lanka is also very explosive. Social divisions between the Sinhalese and Tamils are affecting politics of the country and have brought it in a civil war situation. (2)

In a democracy, political parties would talk to these divisions, ask for votes on this basis, make different promises to the people and talk of politics to redress the grievances of the disadvantaged communities. (1)

17. Women still lag much behind men in India despite some improvements since independence. There are some factors to analyse the given statement:

(i) Literacy Rate : The literacy rate among women is only 64.6% compared with 80.9% among men. A smaller proportion of girls go for higher studies. (1)

(ii) Low Sex – Ratio : Parents in India prefer to have sons. They also find ways to abort the girl child before she is born. Such sex–selective abortion has resulted in a decline in female child sex-ratio. (1)

(iii) Political Representation : In India, women representation in legislature has been very low, while in America, England etc, women are given seats in Parliament even though there are male members. (1)

18. Formal sources of credit are beneficial in the sense that they provide credit at reasonable rates without any undue exploitative practices as faced under informal sources of credit. Importance of formal source of credit:

(i) The formal source of credit includes loan from banks and co–operatives. (½)

(ii) RBI supervises the functioning of formal sources of loans. (½)

(iii) RBI ensures that loans are given not only to the profit – making business man and traderss but also to small–cultivators, small–scale industries, small borrowers etc. (½)

(iv) Banks and co–operative societies need to lend more. This would lead to higher incomes and many people could then borrow cheaply for a variety of needs. They could grow crops, do business, set up small–industries etc. (1)

(v)   Cheap and affordable credit by the formal sector is crucial for the country's development.   (½)

OR

Informal sources of credit are the moneylenders, traders, employers, relatives and friends. There are some bad effects of informal sources of credit:

(i)   The borrowers tend to find themselves in a debt–trap   (½)

(ii)   The rate of interest can be really high as it depends on the wishes of the lender.   (½)

(iii)   There is no organization to supervise its lending activities.   (½)

(iv)   The cost to the borrower becomes much higher that leads to less incomes.   (½)

Section C

19. In India, roadways have preceded railways. They still have an edge over railways in view of the ease with which they can be built and maintained. The growing importance of road transport vis–a–vis rail transport is rooted in the following reasons:

(i)   Construction cost of roads is much lower than that of railways lines.   (1)

(ii)   Roads can traverse comparatively more dissected and undulating topography.   (1)

(iii)   Roads can negotiate higher gradients of slopes and as such can traverse mountains such as the Himalayas.   (1)

(iv)   Road ways tend to provide door to door service, therefore the cost of loading and unloading is much lower.   (1)

(v)   Road transport is economical in transportation of few persons and small amount of goods over short distances.   (1)

20. Belgium is a small country in Europe while Sri Lanka is an island nation is Asia. In Sri Lanka and Belgium, there were ethnic conflicts for power on the basis of the language.   (1)

Belgium has a population of a little over one crore, about half the population of Haryana. whereas Sri Lanka has about two crore people, about the same as in Haryana.   (1)

People of Belgium practice Christianity while people of Sri Lanka follow Buddhism. Out of Belgium's total population. 59% lives in Flemish region and speaks Dutch language and another 40% lives in Wallonia region and speak French while Sri Lankan social groups are Sinhala – speakers and Tamil speakers.

In Belgium, the Dutch community has advantage of its numeric majority and could forced its will on the French and German speaking population. In Sri Lanka, the Sinhala community enjoyed an even bigger majority and could imposed its will on the entire country.   (3)

OR

It is true that the idea of power sharing emerged in opposition to the notions of undivided political power. In modern democracies, power sharing arrangements can take many forms.

Power is shared among different organs of government such as legislature, executive and Judiciary Power can be shared among governments at different levels. A general government for the entire country and governments at the provincial or regional level.   (2)

Power may also be shared among different social groups such as the religious and linguistic groups. 'Community government' in Belgium is a good example of this arrangement.

Power sharing arrangements can also be seen in the way political parties, pressure groups and movements control or influence those in power. In a democracy, the citizens must have freedom to choose among various contenders for power. (3)

21. Although industries contributes significantly to India's economic growth and development, the increase in pollution of land, water, air, noise and resulting degradation of environment that they have caused cannot be overlooked.

   (i) **Air Pollution :** It is caused by the presence of high proportion of undesirable gases, such as sulphur dioxide and carbon monoxide. Air–borne particulate materials contain both solid and liquid particles like dust, sprays mist and smoke. (1)

   (ii) **Water Pollution :** It is caused by organic and inorganic industrial wastes and affluents discharged into rivers. The main culprits in this regard are paper, pulp, chemical textile and dyeing, petroleum refineries, tanneries and electroplating industries that let out dyes, detergents, acids, salts and heavy metals like lead and mercury pesticides (1)

   (iii) **Thermal Pollution :** Thermal pollution of water occurs when hot water from factories and thermal plants is drained into rivers and ponds before cooling. (1)

   (iv) **Noise Pollution :** Noise pollution not only results in hearing impairment, increased heart rate and blood pressure among other physiological effects. (1)

   (v) **Pollution from Nuclear Power Plants :** It causes cancers, birth defects etc, which is life – threatening. (1)

22. Dr. B.R. Ambedkar sought reservation for dalits in educational institutions. For him, political empowerment was the only way of achieving upliftment for dalits. Dr. B.R. Ambedkar and other dalit leaders demanded separate electorates for the depressed classes in order to protect their interest and extending political power to them. Dr. B.R. Ambedkar formed the depressed classes Association in 1930 and demanded the following:

   (i) To bring about political empowerment of the depressed classes. (½)

   (ii) To have reserved seats in the educational institutions. (½)

   (iii) He also mooted the idea of reservation for dalits which brought him in clash with Gandhi. (1)

   (iv) Demanded separate electorates and bring about social justice. (1)

   (v) It was with Ambedkar's constant persuasion which was eventually resolved with the Poona Pact of 1932, which provided for reserved seats in Provincial and central Legislatures for them. (1)

   (vi) He also launched Kaiaram temple movement that sought entry of dalit in the Brahmin dominated temples. (1)

OR

The civil Disobedience Movement led by M.K. Gandhi, in the year 1930 was an important milestone in the history of Indian Nationalism, it began with Gandhi's famous salt march of about 240 miles from Sabarmati Ashram in Ahmedabad to the costal town of dandi in Gujarat.

(i)　Civil Disobedience Movement was one of the most significant movement launched by Mahatma Gandhi where people were asked not only to refuse co–operation but also to break colonial laws. (1)

(ii)　The rich peasants became enthusiastic supporters of the civil disobedience movement participating in the boycott programmes. (1)

(iii)　For the rich peasants, the fight was a struggle against high revenue. (1)

(iv)　The poorer peasants were not just interested in the lowering of the revenue demand but also wanted the unpaid rent to the landlords to be remitted. (1)

(v)　Apprehensive of raising issues that might upset rich peasants, the congress was unwilling to support 'no rent' campaigns in most places. (1)

23. Indian trade has played a crucial role in the late nineteenth century world economy which can be explained as:

(i)　Export of raw cotton from India increased from 5 % to 35 %. (½)

(ii)　Indigo used for dyeing clothes was another important export for many decades. (½)

(iii)　Opium shipment to china grew rapidly to become India's single largest export. (1)

(iv)　Money earned through the sale of opium was used to finance its tea and other imports from china. (1)

(v)　Britain had a 'Trade Surplus' with India Britain used this surplus to balance trade deficit with other countries resulting in multilateral settlement. (1)

(vi)　Food grains and raw material export from India to Britain and rest of the world increased. (1)

OR

A series of changes affected the pattern of industrialization in India by the early twentieth century due to various reasons. They are

(i)　**Swadeshi Movement :** Swadeshi and Boycott movement provided impetus to Indian industries leading to higher demand of Indian goods. (1)

(ii)　**Formation of Business Association :** Formation of FICCI also helped them to protect their collective interest against increasing tariff. (1)

(iii)　**Decline of Indian Goods to China :** It was due to production of cotton goods rather than yarn. (1)

(iv)　**Impact of World War I:** World war I created a different situation where import to India declined as the British factories were producing to meet the war needs. (1)

(v)　At the same time, Indian factories were called upon to supply war needs such as jute bags, clothes and shoes etc. (1)

Hence these changes resulted in creation of resilient and sustainable industrial growth to meet the domestic demand.

OR

Industrialization changed the form of urbanization in the modern period.

(v)   Road transport is economical in t

(i)   The early industrial cities of Britains such as Leeds and Manchester attracted large number of migrants to the textile mills set up in the late 18th century.   (1)

(ii)   London was a colossal city and its population expanded four–fold from 1 million to 4 million, as the Industrial revolution attracted more and more people.   (1)

(iii)   The city of London was a powerful magnet for migrant populations, even though it did not have large factories.   (1)

(iv)   Apart from the London Dock yards, five major types of industries employed large numbers: Clothing and footwear, wood and furniture, metals and engineering, printing and stationery and precision products such as surgical instruments, watches and objects of precious metals.   (1)

(v)   During the first world war (1914–18), London began manufacturing motor cars and electrical goods and the number of large factories increased until they accounted for nearly one–third of all jobs in the city.   (1)

24. Democracy is a better form of government than other alternatives because:

(i)   **Promotes Equality Among Citizens:** It promotes equality among people by providing equal rights for everyone. It brings social, economic and political equality among all.   (1)

(ii)   **Enhances the Dignity of the Individual :** Democracy provides rights for the protection of disadvantageous group where by dignity of every individual irrespective of any differences is upheld.   (1)

(iii)   **Improves the quality of decision making :** Decision making takes place through debate, discussion and deliberation leading to quality decision making.   (1)

(iv)   **Provides a method to resolve conflict :** Conflict and disagreement is obvious in multi-cultural society but these conflicts can be resolved through constitutional and democratic means.   (1)

(v)   **Allows room to correct mistakes :** Democracy enshrines a system of check and balance which allows timely rectification of mistakes if any.   (1)

(vi)   Democracy provides an accountable and responsible government.   (1)

25. There are five facilities available in the Special Economic Zones developed by the central and state governments to attract foreign investment:

(i)   Single window clearance for setting up of a Special Economic Zone.   (1)

(ii)   Exemption from Import duty.   (1)

(iii)   Five years tax holiday (Income Tax).   (1)

(iv)   Liberalizsation in labour laws and availability of skilled and semi–skilled labour forces.   (1)

(v)   Will connected with the network of transport and communication.   (1)

SECTION D

26. (a) $(2 \times 1 = 2)$

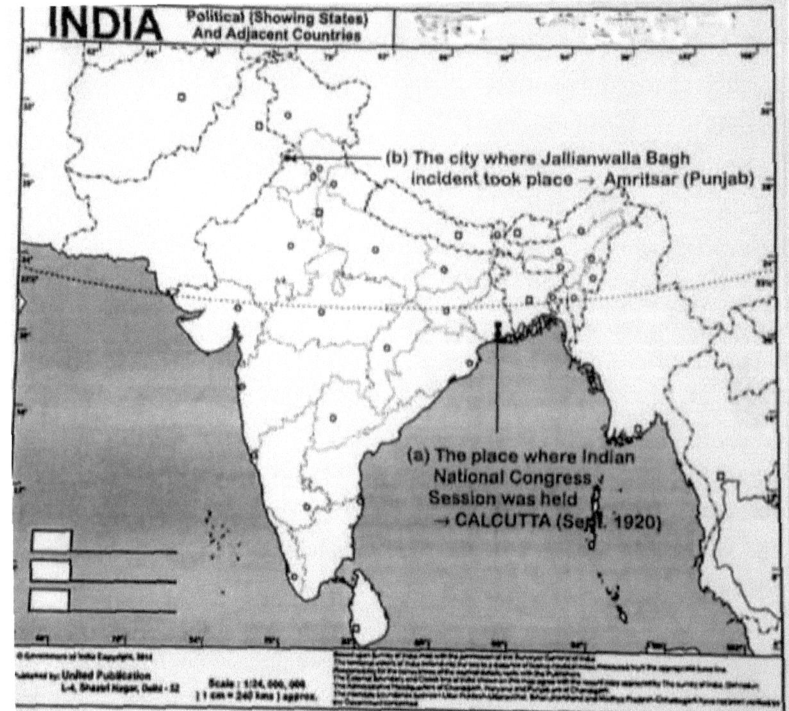

(b) $(3 \times 1 = 3)$

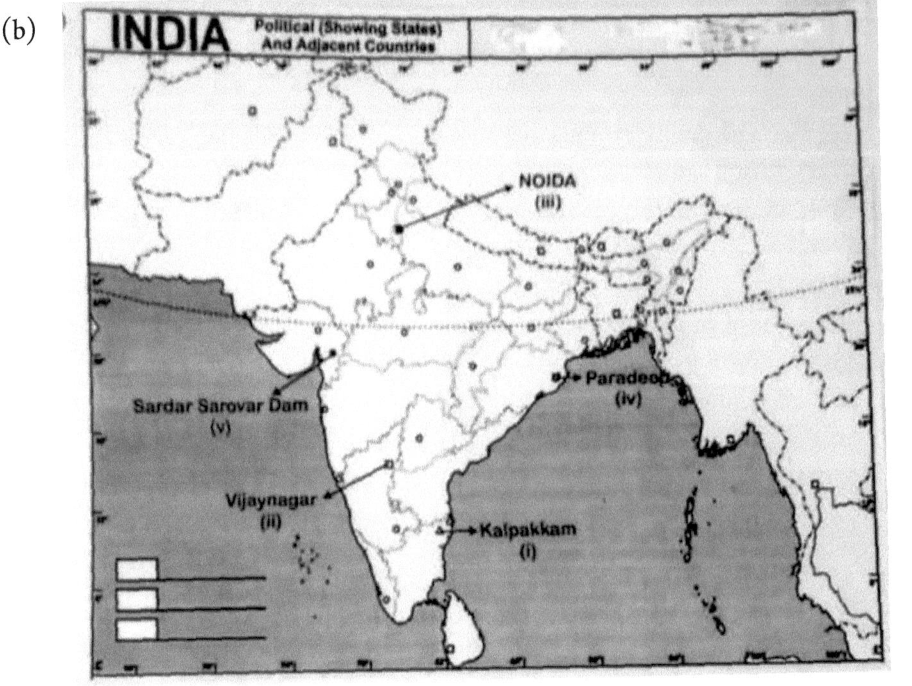

Printed by Libri Plureos GmbH in Hamburg, Germany